SERVE TO PROFIT

*Dedicated to present
and future generations*

SERVE TO PROFIT
Butterfly Leadership

By Tina Monberg with Gitte Larsen (ed.)

© 2014 TINA MONBERG

Editor: Gitte Larsen, Editions/House of Futures
Illustrations and layout: Stine Skøtt Olesen, Nxt/House of Futures
Translation: Dominc Balmforth, Susturb

ISBN: 978-87-997865-0-3

Revised edition

Printed in 100 copies in Danmark by Scandinavian Book

Profit from sales goes to:
Straagaarden
Bregnerødvej 8, Bregnerød
DK - 3250 Gilleleje
info@straagaarden.dk
www.straagaarden.dk

TINA MONBERG
with Gitte Larsen (ed.)

SERVE TO PROFIT

Butterfly Leadership

PRAISE FOR THE BOOK

"Astute leaders recognize that the old paradigm of thinking no longer serves us as individuals, nor as businesses, public organizations, or society as a whole. Today, at this critical juncture, we need a fresh perspective that empowers us to take wise action. Tina Monberg's book, Serve to Profit, generously offers us a way forward. With humility and heart, she brings new light to our past experience and guides us toward the emerging future with a sage's clarity. I came away deeply inspired by The Butterfly and its potential to revolutionize our capacity as leaders to create a positive impact on the world – truly, the simplicity on the other side of complexity." *– Jason C. Meek, CEO, The iDeal World, Lecturer, University of California Berkeley School of Law and formerly, Mediator to the OECD*

"There isn't anything the world needs more than companies paying attention to and serving the whole. It is good for both our inner and our outer worlds. We will experience radical changes in the decades to come – and this calls for new leadership and a new responsibility from all of us. I warmly recommend Tina Monberg's book as a good starting point for the necessary changes in organization and leadership." *– Steen Hildebrandt, Professor emeritus, Organisation and Leadership, Aarhus University*

Contents

PLANET AND PEOPLE

"...The only myth that is going to be worth thinking about in the immediate future is one that is talking about the planet, not the city, not these people, but the planet, and everybody on it. And what it will have to deal with will be exactly what all myths have dealt with—the maturation of the individual, from dependency through adulthood, through maturity, and then to the exit; and then how to relate to this society and how to relate this society to the world of nature and the cosmos... And this would be the philosophy for the planet, not for this group, that group, or the other group. When you see the earth from the moon, you don't see any divisions there of nations or states. This might be the symbol, really, for the new mythology to come."

– Power of Myth interview with mythologist Joseph Campbell

Preface

"The Doomsday Clock" is a symbolic clockface to show how close the human race is to extinction. It was conceived in 1947 by the board members of the Bulletin of the Atomic Scientists at the University of Chicago. Midnight represents the end: annihilation by atomic war or natural catastrophe. The clock was set at seven minutes to midnight during the Cold War and since then, the hands have been pushed forward or backwards depending on the world's current course towards disaster.

In January 2012, the clock was set to five minutes to midnight. This position stayed constant throughout 2013. The board's decision to move closer to midnight was based on the inability of global leaders to tackle the many threats which face us. Professor Lawrence Krauss elaborates on the board's decision with this explanation:

Unfortunately Einstein's words of 1946, 'everything has changed except for our way of thinking', still hold true. The positive developments predicted for these last two years never happened. This justified our decision in putting the clock forward to its 2007 position. In the context of present and real dangers; the accumulation of atomic weapons, climate change, a pressure to find safe and sustainable energy sources, etc., global leaders have not been able to change business as usual. A general passivity in relation to these central issues provides the motivation for movement on the clockface. As we see it, the greatest threat to human life in the 21st Century is how to meet the global energy demand created by the growth in both developing countries and industrial societies, without causing further climatic damage, without increasing the international arsenal of atomic weapons, and without subjecting people to a loss in their health and community. What we miss amidst all this, is any real focus and action to prepare a new context for global reductions.

The bad news and the good news
The bad news is the position of the clock-hands on the Doomsday Clock.

The good news is that we can change this position.

The global leaders referred to by the board includes both political and business leaders. Together, we can create the necessary changes to overcome the multiple crises we are experiencing. At the 2013 World Economic Forum in Davos, Switzerland, some of the world's largest companies described the near future as a "transformation". Many declared, for the first time, that there was no going back to *"business as usual."*

This book presents a systematic vision for a future which can contain both sustainability and growth, terms often described in opposition to one another, though they needn't be. Most companies aim exclusively towards generating the largest possible economic profit. A few others operate as exclusively socially responsible companies with the aim of only doing good. This book reveals a third way, one where social responsibility and profit are not opposites, but on the contrary can complement and support one another a path where the three P's - People, Planet and Profit - go hand in hand and create healthy, resilient purpose.

We find ourselves in a time where change is simply the condition of everyday life. The faster the world changes, the more we need to challenge our own beliefs. This requires a flexibility in company structure and leadership that we haven't yet seen. We can no longer navigate as supertankers but instead as small, fast moving dinghies.

The new Nordic way

"The strength of a small country lies in its unity."
Carl Gustaf Mannerheim, former Finnish president

In order to navigate as small and responsive dinghies, we must rediscover Nordic values such as trust, authenticity, openness, interdependency, community, and social responsibility. These values offer a unique starting point for a more sustainable form of development. The flat hierarchy which is common to Nordic companies and organisations harbours initiative and responsibility amongst both leaders and employees alike. A flat organizational structure creates a tradition for dialogue and a more informal way of working together. The Nordic countries are well equipped to contribute positively to the transformations we see occuring globally. As such, they can seize the opportunity to actually do something about it.

To make money, make the whole

This book will provide you with an insight into the Nordic universe of trust, equality, inclusion, flexibility, respect for nature and a high degree of work ethic. The Nordic culture of strong dialogues between stakeholders creates an environment of flexibility and an understanding for the bigger picture. It also creates balance between the company and the individual.

This book will challenge you as a leader and help steer your course within an uncertain future giving you the overview of what lies within our grasp. Once we know where we stand, it is then easier to act and discover new ways forward; new opportunities for more life and more meaning. We must rediscover the whole, now lacking within the current system devised from details and silo-thinking. The more that companies function like the natural world, the more resilient they, and, resultantly, we, become.

This book reveals three core design parameters which give shape to nature; namely flow, flexibility and form. These show us a model for self-organisation which can teach volumes to a company's mission, structure and success. This model results in growth, integration and sustainability; three fundamental qualities for setting a company free and for granting a new ability to navigate.

You will be presented with companies that manage to create the whole *whilst* creating profit. Companies that dare to trash budgets and control. Companies that don't have size as a goal, but maneuverability. Companies that dare to grant their employees free rein, and where decentralisation is a goal in itself. Companies that define their success relative to the good function of the society in which they operate. Companies that have already recognised they will not reach success in rigid silos.

Interviews with specific business leaders in Denmark and Sweden support the ideas we put forward and position them in a real context. These leaders are not only case examples of a particular line of thought. They have chosen paths of their own. As such, the interviews are stories about unique individuals, each with a deep respect for the world they do business in. They are leaders with clear visions, belief in their own abilities, and at the same time humility and respect for those who have worked to realise their goal.

Let us break the silos down and instead create a new company and leadership model, where growth and sustainability are no longer at loggerheads but coupled together as an integrated movement. The model is based on a three-fold structure for collaboration and leadership: *servant leadership, facilitation* and *personal leadership.* We need leaders to create the framework and employees to create the content. We need organisation and collaboration to be considered as an ongoing process which is constantly directed towards creating sustainable growth.

The book is divided into three parts which you will be guided through in order to allow for a successful transformation in business thinking. I invite you to be the next one who takes the leap. The formula is simple:

1. Tear down the silos
2. Build up the platforms
3. Set the movement free!

Tina Monberg
Copenhagen, August 2014

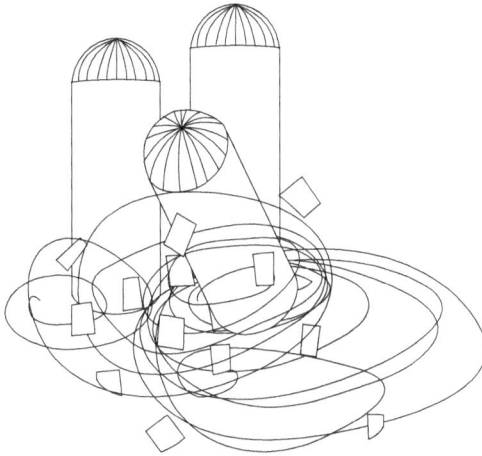

Part I: TEAR DOWN THE SILOS

"We resist seeking the illusory comfort
of certainty and stability."

– Margaret Wheatley

"In our imaginary cells we hold
the impulse of a better world."

– Barbara Marx Hubbard

WHAT ARE YOU DOING?

Long ago, a man is hiking through France. At one point, he meets a mason and asks, "What are you doing?" The mason looks up. He replies crossly, "I am breaking these stones with my hammer and chisel. Then, I put them at my side for someone else to pick up and take away. My back hurts and it's too hot to work. It's a boring job which I have no desire to do." After a while the hiker meets another mason and asks him the same question, "What are you doing?" The man looks up and answers, "I have a wife and children. They need food, so I need to earn the money to support them. I am breaking these stones so that I can buy bread for tonight's dinner." The traveller continues on his way and before long meets a third mason. He asks him the same question, " What are you doing?" The third mason looks up at him with a glint in his eye and replies, "I'm building a cathedral".

– A traveller's tale

CHAPTER 1

Isolated in silos

"Why the hell would you stand by a runway lugging baggage around if you didn't understand that bringing baggage safely to its destination is part of building the cathedral?". These are the words of Jan Carlzon, former CEO for Scandinavian Airlines (SAS). The question here concerns whether or not people know *why* they do what they do.

Our desire for control and security has driven us to rigid structures that no longer fulfil our real needs. We are locked in the conviction that people want only to protect their own interests rather than the collective interest. We think that leadership becomes more efficient when we take charge of everything, right down to the smallest detail. In fact, this results only in us stressing out in our own silo. We conduct isolated lives, with neither perspective nor direction.

This the problem covered in Part 1.

Silo-thinking creates fragmentation

Silo or blinkered-thinking can be traced back to the farms storage silos, where it was important not to mix the different corn types and keep them separate. Today, the silo is a well known metaphor for the way we divide and specialise work and business. The silo is perceived as creating good order and a good overview by dividing and simplifying something that would otherwise appear unmanageable. For top management, well-defined segments give a more organised overview of the whole. As such, they are in a better position to steer the tasks which they allocate to individual departments. Or so it seems.

In fact, when applied to business, silos contain several inborn and fundamental problems. Whereas the silo can accommodate internal knowledge sharing, it is a highly obstructive environment for knowledge sharing between and across departments.

When the departments of a company or organisation don't share knowledge, the prospect of success and even long-term survival is significantly reduced. The kind of mentality that belongs to silo-thinking lowers a company's morale and operational efficiency, and undermines the chance of harbouring a productive business culture. Silos often create a fragmented reality where one can only see the individual parts of the company and not the whole.

There are numerous examples of this. For instance, when a sales department promises a delivery to the customer which the production department cannot meet. The sales department is rewarded for increasing orders, whilst the production department can only receive bad will for not being able to keep up. When a customer expresses their dissatisfaction with a late delivery, and are told that this isn't the fault of the sales person, but of distribution. When a telephone company employee openly shares with the customer their own disagreement with a management decision to withdraw the option for instore payment.

Another problem with silos is the endless struggle to record all activities, rules, and mechanisms which everyday operation demands. The question is whether the silo structure in fact fulfils our desire for certainty and security, or whether our attempt to register all possible activities is thwarted. Regardless of how diligently we record such activities, we can never collect the full description because there are living people in the silo who are in a constant state of change and flux. In practice, we can risk that as soon as a problem's parameters have been analysed and noted the original situation or context has since changed entirely. A new unregistered set of problems arises and we are left grappling blindly for solutions.

Even if we are successful in demolishing silos, they can rise again as fast as they were removed, unless we introduce something else in their place. The reason for the silos being here in the first place is still alive and well. We need structure around us in order not to end in chaos. Assens, a small town in Denmark, witnessed just how resilient silos can be when two sugar silos, no longer serving their purpose, were earmarked for demolition. When the noise and smoke had settled after detonating the first silo, it was left standing, four metres shorter, but otherwise unscathed. Experts were called in but were unable to offer a reasonable explanation. Some experts believed that the silo was built with an inner layer which gave it its unsual strength, but which couldn't be seen at first glance. It was first a week later, when the neighbours had moved to a hotel to avoid being hit by the silo falling in on itself, that the demolition team were successful in blowing both towers up.

Self-interest and all against all

In 1776, the Scottish economist, Adam Smith, wrote about the phenomenon of *'the invisible hand'* in his seminal work, 'The Wealth of Nations'. This provided an image of a natural market mechanism which steers and ensures free movement and competition. The idea is that if the individual consumer can choose freely what to buy and if the producer can choose freely what to make and sell, then the market will, of its *own* accord, select the right product, distribution and price to suit everyone. This model suggests that a mutually beneficial environment for commerce is created as a result of self interest.

This belief has severed strong roots in western business culture and we experience it in numerous ways in current times. For example, businesses set personal targets for employees in order to motivate them to fulfil their own success criteria. This is explained by Adam Smith as follows:

It is not from the butcher, brewer or baker's good will that we should expect our next dinner, but from acknowledgement of their own self interest. We appeal not to their love for the greater good but to the love they hold for themselves. We don't speak of our own needs but rather of their benefit.

Adam Smith's thinking is not wrong, but incomplete and out of date. It is based on two assumptions. The first, that people want only to care for their own needs.

The American psychologist, Abraham H. Maslow (1908-1970) was founder of a *humanistic psychology* based on the view that people should be considered as whole beings, in their entirety. If, for a moment, we consider Marlow's famous pyramid of human needs (see fig. 2 on page 62), then the assumption that we only care for own well being, puts us at the bottom of the pyramid and keeps us there. It is in this part of the pyramid that we have our essential, basic needs - physiological needs, needs for safety and security. Even though a great number of the world's population still lack these basic needs, Western cultures have, despite economic crises, moved progressively upwards in the pyramid. The top half describes our so-called growth needs, including needs for self-realization and altruism. People are social creatures. We need to contribute to a larger gathering than ourselves and we know instinctively that this is beneficial for our own survival.

The other assumption in Smith's thinking is that people are only motivated by higher income. But, in this postmodern era, we are driven by other, higher aims. We now seek deeper meaning in our work. Adam Smith described a system for growth without referring to the undesirable by-products of a free market system or the social nature of people which since the end of the 1960s and in particular the 1970s has played a key role in the discussion. In 1973, E.F Schumacher released his famous book, "Small Is Beautiful; A Study of Economics As If People Mattered" in which he argues for durability over efficiency and speed. A system's ability to last - to sustain itself - was far more important to him than it was to Adam Smith. Schumacher writes: "From an economic perspective, wisdom's key concept is longevity. We should study economy's longevity."

The conflict between growth and sustainability is by no means new, but we have yet to find new systems and structures that can accommodate both.

Industrialisation's mechanical approach to production and productivity strives towards fastest, cheapest and best. The company is a machine, and if a component, department or employee fails to function at its best, then it must be replaced for the machine to continue. The silos function as separate, well-oiled machines, each work perfectly by themselves, but which have difficulty sharing information and knowledge or working together. If you work in silo A, you hold no responsibility for the activities in silo B. If you take on the tasks of silo B, you are not paid for doing this and may also be punished for getting involved in the work of others. In a well-functioning machine, all components are known and all the different functions are described in detail. Everyone knows what is expected of them in each silo. It is in no one's interest to unleash the power of integration or innovation which can arise from collaborating.

The US Space Shuttle Challenger disaster of 1986 is a historic example of a lack of cooperation and knowledge exchange between silos. The American president gave a team of investigators 120 days to discover the technical failure that had caused the accident. In his book, Challenger – A Technical Accident, Claus Jensen writes:

"The commission found the failure, but in doing so, they revealed a lot more than technical negligence in the course of their investigation. System failures, quick cover-ups, and the many tensions present in rival company cultures began appearing throughout. It became increasingly difficult to draw a ring around the extent of the cause and furthermore, to guarantee both the President and the population that the Challenger accident couldn't repeat itself in a modern, industrialised society."

When something goes wrong in an organisation, we look for the cause of the problem so that we can put it right. Challenger exploded with a huge bang in the sky as a symbol of failure for mechanical, industrial thinking. This was not a one-off event. Similar explosions, albeit of smaller scale, occur regularly in all companies in which cross-company dialogue and cooperation aren't happening. We think that we have a good overview when we are able to describe our companies down to the smallest detail. This illusion is a key driver of our mechanised world view.

In physics, researchers have been searching for the smallest building block of all matter which makes the universe, in order to understand the whole. This search has dug deeper and deeper, without reaching the bottom. The smallest entity known by physics today is the **quark.** A proton consists of, for example, three quarks and the quark only exists as a triad of two up-quarks and one down-quark. The down-quark is the mediator, because it sets up the link between the other two quarks. In nature, certain forms of life can only exist in partnership with others. Companies and organisations can learn a lot from this. All living systems have an inborn, natural *flow*, but silos with their thick outer walls block this flow. Now is the time for us to widen our view such that we can understand the full picture of a functional living system.

No system can work without growth, and when we don't have growth, we die. This is the way many politicians and business leaders think. Growth is an inevitable part of nature's order, but so too is transformation. Nothing stands still. All is in motion. Life is diverse. With our primary focus on growth as an isolated economic phenomenon, we have lost track of sustainability and cohesiveness. When growth becomes one-dimensional, it behaves as a form of cancer that eats everything around it. The cancer isn't aware that its behaviour is also the cause of its own downfall since the body it feeds off will eventually die of exhaustion.

With the economic focus we have today, we act as masters of nature. In reality, our economic system is just one part of a much larger biological and natural system. In his book, Profit for Life, Joseph H. Bragdon describes how we must prioritise living assets - people and nature - over and above non-living assets - machines and capital - since everything living is a precondition for the non-living. If businesses don't do this they die. Bragdon's many years of research on and in a wide range of companies, demonstrates that the companies who prioritise the living over the non-living achieve better economic results.

He calls this, "*Living Asset Stewardship*", and to practise it, a company must adopt a decentralised management and network structure which is based on self-initiative, cooperation and trust. A company culture should be characterised by a *serving* leadership, in which the leader's role is to strenghten the employee's professional development, and where everyone wants to keep learning and gaining new skills. When creating an innovative environment, it is important to allow space for experiment and for making mistakes. Furthermore, Bragdon stresses the need for a caring financial management which demonstrates a clear intention to employ sustainable policies which, in the long term, can support future generations.

Isolated in silos – *Summary*
To breathe life into the silos, we must balance a short-term and growth-based drive to be biggest, best, and cheapest, with a consideration for community and long term sustainability — more on that in the next chapter. Only by valuing both the needs of the individual and the whole, can we grow and survive, long term.

- We have been driven by a need for security and overview, which we thought could only be achieved by micromanaging the details in our system. This has lead to fragmentation.
- The deeper we immerse ourselves in such details, the less perspective we have. We have lost the image of wholeness. We have lost the meaning and understanding of integration and continuity.
- To keep our system running, we build on a mechanistic understanding and consider people as separate elements rather than as whole beings in relation to and connected to each other.
- Our economic theories are based on the idea that we are egoistic creatures, that we are exclusively driven by the will to fulfil our own needs and therefore only guard the interests of our own individual silo.

INTRO

SAS introduced a dentralised model to their business, years ago when Jan Carlzon was leading the company. It is exactly this model that I advocate in this book. After Carlzon had written "Riv pyramiderne ned" ("Tear the Pyramids Down"), everyone tried to do it, but often ended up putting up new silos in their place.

A passion for goal setting

Jan Carlzon once said: "Those who have not been given the right information, cannot take responsibility. Delegating without giving people the prerequisites for independent decision-making leads nowhere." But given the right information people will be set free.

This is, according to Carlzon, the "Nordic Secret", and the reason why Nordic organisations are successful at decentralization and releasing high levels of Nordic trust capital. Carlzon has been criticized for his passion for goal-setting as larger goals help us see beyond our daily tasks, but for him, the only correct way to organise SAS when he became CEO in 1981 was decentralization.

In this interview he explains the way to decentralization: "The most important is not actually a decentralized organisation. This is not a goal in itself. More vital is the force coming from the customer and directed towards the employee, who is there to serve the customer. Both myself and Jan Wallander from Handelsbanken realised back then that our only resource lay in fulfilling the needs of the customer. The organisation part almost comes by itself when the key question we keep asking ourselves is, how to be most useful and most valuable to the customer. The answer is not necessarily the same for two different people. So what is good service? This is determined by the meeting between two people. When serving the customer, I must be able to read their needs from one moment to the next and constantly adjust my service to suit. This is the simple explanation for why it simply doesn't work with a centralized organisation, where top management decides to offer the same service to everyone. The moment I meet the customer and offer my service is the moment of truth. It is of course therefore that I entitled my book. "Moments of Truth". The boundary between good and bad service may be only a few millimeters."

Do you also think that the decentralized organisation you created for SAS was particularly Nordic?
"Absolutely. We discovered that the decentralized culture worked well throughout the world, but had most difficulty being accepted in the USA. Here, one is used to a much more hierarchical approach, where it is common practice to delegate upwards and thereby dodge responsibility if something goes wrong. I think that my approach to leadership coincides with the key characteristics of the Scandinavian countries. Solidarity amongst people in the same organisation, respect for the individual and support for those weaker or less well off. This made it easier for us, as a company, to create a decentralized culture at all levels and in all departments – since all this was already present in society. We spoke and thought in the same way, but I have to say, we have a challenge on our hands in Scandinavia right now with the indoctrination of American culture via film and TV concepts such as Topmodel, Robinson etc. These are degrading and disrespectful to the individual and show no collective spirit."

How was the philsophy for "helping the weak" practised in reality at SAS?
"This could be seen, for example, if someone didn't succeed in their particular job. It didn't follow that the person involved would prove unable to do any task but rather that they were perhaps better suited in another role. Or if an employee simply didn't match our company, we could still help them to move on to somewhere or something else. When I read articles today about mass layoffs, I think how important it is not to be too tough, but to always remember empathy and respect."

You have said that the kind of organisation you created demanded a lot of control – isn't there a contradiction here?
"For me, this is a sign of respect. If you put responsibility on several thousand people, this then requires more follow-up, and more feedback. This means that, as a leader, I must bear my part of the responsibility. If I have expectations of you, as an employee, to carry out certain tasks, then I show you most respect when I give you constructive feedback, and let you know if things aren't good. This also gives employees the chance to correct whatever is deemed unsatisfactory".

How was it to come to SAS in 1981 and launch the new mindset?
"SAS was in crisis, but was still focused heavily on developing technology. In contrast to this, I believed that we were forced to turn the focus on people. Thus arose the sentence "We have learnt to fly aeroplanes, now we need to learn to fly people." This is another mindset all together.

How could you communicate this in a conscious way to top management and the board of directors?
"It is true that I have been very conscious of making sure people not only understood the message but also felt its value. I stood up and said that our focus should be on business travel. As such we should offer business-class customers a separate check-in, more departures, and fewer, but more direct flights. So, I said, all this will involve investment in new products, amounting to hundreds of millions of kroner. In the same year as the company was about to go bankrupt, I suggested that we invest large sums of money. But, at the same time, I declared personal responsibility for next year's results hitting positive figures. Only at this point, could we begin to discuss how to cut expenditure, because until this point we wouldn't know whether or not the new initiatives had worked or which ones proved profitable. We couldn't start by cutting expenses. This was how it had to be. One could say that SAS were forced into either saying yes, in which case I had full responsibility, or saying no, and watching me walk out the door."

What about middle-management? They too needed to go through the transformation of decentralizing.

"We told middle-management that we were upturning the traditional model in which middle-management passed on instructions issued to them by top-management. The entire role of middle-management changed, demanding them to answer directly to customer needs and support those at front desk who held the majority of face to face encounters. In the hierarchy of a traditional business, an employee in a service function is seen as having a lower status than one issuing orders. But here, we moved all the pieces around. Many of the middle-management adapted to suit, but many others made blockages in opposition. Actually, I don't really know how we could have tackled it better. Perhaps with more education or training. But we had little time to consider this before we found ourselves on a burning platform, at which point it was *make it* or *break it*. Some of those in leadership probably felt they had been driven down, and this wasn't made better by those at front desk seizing the new initiatives like their new religion. Middle management were confronted with those beneath them turning round and saying "Now it's us who decide!" Many of those in positions of authority felt that we had drained them of their power."

When middle-management surrender their power in this new kind of organisation, what role do they take on instead?

"This is difficult. I call this the rockwool layer. If you have been used to giving orders, but are then told suddenly that now the customer decides, you wonder who is left steering the company. The answer is the front-line, that is those with immediate contact with the customer. "

With this said, and when one reads your book, there is some doubt to whether you think you succeeded in bringing middle-management on board.

"Actually, that's why I wrote the book. I knew there were many middle-managers who either didn't understand what

I was saying, or didn't *want* to understand. This was an issue across all categories; pilots, technicians, financial and administrative personnel. I figured that it would help for them to understand, because with no knowledge, comes no responsibility."

Do you think that this challenge with middle-management would have resolved itself had there been more time?
"I think it would have helped if I had used more time and development on revising people's service roles and ability to communicate. It's all about gaining a greater understanding."

When you look back, what could you have done differently?
I could have left SAS in 1988. At this time I had succeeded in making a turnaround, and I'm a turnaround specialist! If myself and the board had had this insight at the time, then we would have said, "Let us stop here and bring in someone to fine tune the business and develop middle-management". I believe that each period has its own leadership. At one point, I thought about writing a sequel to *Moments Of Truth* called, *Moments of Danger*. Visionary leaders can become extremely dangerous as soon as their mission is complete.

My mission was done once we had become the highest earning airline in the world, and the best airline in the world for business travel. We were awarded best international airline in 1982 and again in 1986. We couldn't get higher. I should perhaps have quit here. Instead, it was just me and not the rest of SAS who would carry the banner for the next new vision. I stood up there and presented the vision, saying "isn't it fantastic, what we are building here?". I clearly remember a presentation in which one brave guy interrupted, "Stop, stop, Jan. Can't you feel that you're losing us?" At the same time, I gave up the key message of my lectures, that of holding focus on the business part. I began moving in the opposite direction and diverting into all kinds of different fields."

How did it influence your own life?
"I remember 1991 as a really tough year. It all went in the wrong direction. It was the same year that Saddam Hussein moved into Kuwait, which in some ways was worse than 9/11. This year left its mark on me."

"How do you look at things today"
I think that I can be proud of what I did. If nothing else, I did a lot of good for a lot of people. I am often given proof that I have meant a lot for peoples' lives and careers. In the tenth anniversary edition of the Swedish magazine, *Chef*, they asked 1,700 business leaders, which person had had the biggest impact on their own development. 48 percent replied, *"Jan Carlzon"*. Of course, I listen to and accept this kind of recognition. I feel that I have made an impact."

WHICH SYSTEM TO FEED?

An old Cherokee Native American is teaching his grand-son about life. "I have an inner fight", he says to the boy and tells of a ferocious battle between two wolves. "One is evil; jealous, vindictive, greedy, arrogant, self-pitying, lying and egocentric. The other wolf is good; gentle, loving, hopeful, trusting, calm, humble, friendly, empathic, generous, truthful and compassionate. The same fight is active in you, and indeed in all people," says the old man. The boy thinks a while and then asks his grandfather, "Which wolf wins?" To which the old man replies; "The one you feed".

– A tale from the Cherokee Native Americans.

CHAPTER 2

Systems should serve us

This chapter is about systems and structures that were originally created because they made sense for another time and in a different society. In particular, this applies to our all encompassing culture of laws and legislation and the whole mindset which goes with it. Only when we understand why and how we hold onto the old systems and silos, and in doing so feed a system which lacks personal responsibility and holistic insight, can we begin to create a new, more sustainable system.

Our systems should serve us

No system exists if it didn't make sense at the time of its creation. All systems and structures are created to serve a purpose or fulfil specific needs. In the first chapter, you read about how the desire for security and control has driven us to a rigid silo-structure which can no longer meet our needs for maneuverability, relationships and cooperation. We, people, are driven by our needs. So when people aren't satisfied with the system they live in, dissatisfaction starts to emerge within and then for the system itself. Dissatisfaction leads us to look around for a new system which can work better for us.

We currently stand in no-man's land. We are already aware that the rigid structures we have created for our companies no longer function effectively. We know that we need to figure out what to replace them with, but at the same time, we have great difficulty in doing so in practice. One of the reasons for this our recognition of the fact that we ourselves are sustaining the very system that we no longer want. We find it very diffcult to decipher the dynamism and complexity of our current system, and it is only by doing this that we can make the transformation.

Change-guru, Professor John Kotter, describes the accumulation of inexpediencies in a system as a *"burning platform"* that should warrant a *"sense of urgency"* and it is precisely this which can guide us towards something new. The speed with which we can build something new, depends not only on our sense for the need to change but also on our own ability to create the new platform. If we are standing on a burning platform and another platform lies in front of us, ready to step onto, the transformation happens without much difficulty. If, on the other hand, there is nothing to step onto; for example, if the new platform doesn't yet exist, we remain in the old system.

The Arab Spring is an example of a burning platform which exploded in November 2010, one man in Tunisia set fire to himself in protest of the way he was treated by the police. This episode led to an uprising that noone saw coming. A large part of the population in Tunisia, Lebanon, Oman and Egypt took to the street to demonstrate against the powers that suppressed them. But the new systems that should replace the old ones weren't implemented quickly enough, and many were killed in the chaos which these countries were thrown into. Military power took over, for example, in Egypt, which resulted in the population being locked in the regime from which they had hoped to escape. Only time can show whether or not Egypt will succeed in creating a well-functioning and democratic society.

Changes within systems occur constantly and often much more subtlety than in the case of Arab Spring. Just as nature doesn't remain static, neither do our systems. They change in order to improve their effectiveness. People explore their environment in search of the optimal system, but at the same time, systems have an inbuilt inertia which opposes transformation. It is in this paradox - between the necessity to find something new and the fear of letting go of what is familiar - that the new is born. New systems often arise from the ruins of an earlier regime. As such, it is useful to uncover the reasons for the old system failing in order to construct the new one.

When a ship is on collision course towards an iceberg, the captain has three choices: he can change course and sail to the left of it; he can change course and sail to the right; or he can choose to do nothing. To do nothing is also a choice. I believe that the world is on direct course towards the iceberg and we must choose a new course now. The crises that face us can only be overcome by us working together. As far as the survival of our species is concerned, we are all in the same boat. We can fight and compete with one another as we head towards the iceberg or we can work together and hope for the best. Perhaps in a hundred years from now, our successors will wonder what on earth we were thinking of, and why it took so long to react to the signals we were given to change course.

We get lost in legislation

In Denmark, a thousand laws were passed each year throughout the 1990's. According to an analysis conducted by the company Kaas & Mulvad and the newspaper A4, we have reached around two thousand new laws and legislations annually (August 2012). This development has happened in spite of the current government's ambition for deregulation. Against their will, they themselves are feeding the growth of a system they no longer want.

The European Union shares Denmark's aim to limit detailed legislation with a policy to *deregulate*. The EU member states recognise that they can no longer lead with legislation due to the ever-increasing amount of knowledge and information which will need to be processed. In the end, the makers become lost in their own laws. Therefore, the EU's plan is to replace detail legislation with framework legislation, whereby those creating the legislation describe its intention and the separate countries then apply the most effective framework. For example, instead of making legislation on the exact curve for a cucumber, all cucumbers are approved whose shape enables easy transportation. Change sounds easy, but it isn't simple to build an entirely new system. Deregulation requires a new mindset and a new way to lead. Employees need to take responsibility for creating the content for any given intention or context.

Despite wanting to do something different, we often end up doing more of the same. We know that more laws won't satisfy our need for responsibility and freedom, but the system is strong and has a tendency to steer us. Why then do we continue to accept something which fails to meet our needs despite the fact that we both see and recognise it's failures?

From an early age, we are brought up with laws as a prerequisite for our existence. We have learnt that the alternative would be chaos. In Denmark, our first law was the Jutland ("*Jyske*") Law of 1241. It is written on the front of the Danish National Courthouse and above the door to the Danish parliament; "*With law will land be built.*" The assumption is that we need written rules to tell us what is right and wrong, and this belief has spread throughout all areas of society. It also applies to business and any organisation which requires a description of working practice and protocol. The trouble with this system is that as soon as one law is implemented we need another. In this way, we get two laws and are left with a gap between them which must be filled with a third to stop us falling between the two existing laws. This, in turn, produces two further holes in the sequence and results in a vicious circle, so that we accumulate more and more laws as time goes on (see figure 1)

When we delve into details, we lose our overview and ability to think for ourselves, which was the whole idea originally with *Jyske Law*:

With law will land be built, but when each one of us can make do with their own and allows others to do the same, then no law is necessary. No law is to be followed as an ultimate truth, but whenever there is doubt about what is true, then the law must show us the truth.

The first law

The fourth law

The third law

The fifth law

The second law

When the second law is passed, this creates a gap between the first and second laws. This gap is filled by the third law, but then we are left with two gaps in the law. These gaps are filled by the fourth and fifth laws but now we have four gaps in the law.

The truth is seen as that which we find most natural and functional for both ourselves and our environment. However, it can be difficult to see the truth from behind the thick walls of the silo, when we lose perspective and meaning. We hide behind rules in order to avoid the responsibility and consequence of our own actions. This way of life actually makes us less intelligent, as individuals, as a business and as a society. We get progressively worse at solving the problems that face us. Rather than serving our own interests and those of society at large, we allow ourselves to be lead by law and legislation. We continue to feed the wrong system, which leaves us not only in a fragmented reality but lost within our own laws. Far too many people don't understand all the laws and sets of procedures, and far too many businesses use endless amounts of time, money, and effort in keeping up with the quantity and pace of new ones being written. There is an acute need to put truth, freedom, and our ability for self-organisation back at the centre. This can only happen when we make a conscious decision to overcome the system's inbuilt inertia. We must decide which wolf we need to feed and perhaps start with simply using our common sense.

"Simplicity is a virtue. Complicated rules prevent progress and lead to bureaucracy. Exaggerated planning is the most common cause of death for a company. That's why simplicity is a tradition for us. Simple routines, simple behaviour, simple life."

- Ingvar Kamprad, IKEA's founder and owner in the book:
"Kamprad´s lilla gulblå" (Kamprad's little yellow-blue)

Before Thomas Woodrow Wilson became President of the United States in 1913, he was Dean of Princeton University. At a meeting, the other professors complained that students kept breaking college rules by walking across the grass between separate buildings. Instead of enforcing the rule, Wilson asked the students why they walked across the grass. He was told, of course, that this was the shortest route between the library and the lecture hall and in response, created a permanent pathway through the grass. I'm sure that you know of situations where the route across the grass is the shortest, and perhaps you choose the short-cut. As individuals and in business, we need to take power back from the system, so that it is us controlling it and not vice versa.

Business leaders must create the new structures
As Karl Marx described it, the *superstructure* always comes after the *base (structure)*, that is, all that happens in society. Detailed laws are constructed from outdated knowledge and often these laws will keep the system we have in operation. The law will, as a rule, appear one-dimensional from our human perspective, which means that we will involuntarily bypass a great deal of important information. There is nothing wrong with a system that behaves completely correctly and predictably. The problem is that there is a constant mass of knowledge and information which falls through the net. One of the most important ingredients for creating new and better systems is the system's own ability to stimulate cooperation and tight bonds between businesses and other parties. We live in an age of extreme complexity with a vast and comprehensive data set and logistical efficiency. Despite

this, none of us can fully comprehend the extent of what we have created. Everyone is trying to keep up to date by using different analysis softwares, but the question is whether or not the key decision-makers are able to gain the knowledge they need to act before the existing system collapses.

In his book, *"The Black Swan"*, Nassim Nicholas Taleb describes how, by analysing the details we know, we miss what is most important: things that we can see afterwards, but which we forgot to look for. Taleb calls this *"The Black Swan"*. The power of what we don't see, and which therefore seems most impossible, is often that which can have the biggest impact. However, this is usually hidden in the wisdom of hindsight. The theory of the black swan describes the disproportionally large effect that rare occurrences can have. Such rare occurrences are hard to predict and lie beyond our normal expectations of history, knowledge, economy and technology. Because of this, we tend not to keep an eye out for them.

Despite the current crises, regarding economy, environment and energy, and which suggest that we should look out for black swans, we keep trying, in western societies, to solve our problems by doing more of what created them. We try to legislate and regulate our way out of crisis, but instead this makes us blind to the bigger picture and unable to see the connection between the different crises.

Some believe that we have time left to act, and that the situation is not yet so critical. Therefore, we don't need to react so drastically in terms of upturning the system we have. Others believe that we can simply repair the existing system or wait until we have a clearer understanding before embarking on large scale change. Many businesses feel that they are in the midst of a storm and that they have neither the energy or courage to carry out large changes to their infrastructure. Their primary concern is to create stability within an uncertain world. Until now, many have assumed that we can simply return to *business as usual,* and to the way things were before the financial crisis, the energy crisis, the climate crisis, the resource crisis, the food crisis and the population crisis. Today, though, more and more of us accept that these multiple crises are not just passing tides. Connie Hedegaard, Climate Commissioner for the European Union, made the following statement to Danish broadsheet, *Information*, in October 2012: "I have said internally to the commission that it is no longer relevant to discuss this economic crisis as if it were just a question of time before we come out the other end of the tunnel and back to where we were before the crisis hit." In other words, we are standing on a burning platform, and we shouldn't expect that our current political and regulatory system can solve the problems for us. Neither can we wait to act until the ground burns around us. Business leaders need to take responsibility for creating new systems and structures which, to a far greater extent, are decentralised and based on self-organisation.

It is not a new idea that businesses have a responsibility to improve global welfare. In January 1971 a group of European business leaders, under the leadership of Klaus Schwab, acting Professor of Business Politics at Geneva University, took the initiative of founding The European Management Forum. In 1987, the name was changed to The World Economic Forum, an independent international organisation responsible for bringing together political, business and academic leaders to address global challenges and global conflicts. Every year, hundreds of such leaders meet at The World Economic Forum in Davos, Switzerland.

We can only use raw materials once
The map we still use to navigate today was created at a time when the world was a very different place. Businesses followed political law and legislation introduced in the context of industrial growth, where the key aim was to be faster, better and cheaper. This is why there is still an inbuilt strategy to grow ourselves out of crisis. More profit means better business. The growth paradigm is based on the assumption that there will always be sufficient raw materials to provide the

input, and that those businesses which tap these resources most efficiently will win. The problem, though, is there isn't sufficient resources to maintain this course, and as such we should begin to turn our focus on the black swans.

With industrialisation, we saw a dramatic increase in the need for laws and ways to implement these laws, for example via accounts. When we look at the balance sheet behind a company's success, the raw materials, which the company extracts from the earth, are listed as income instead of capital. Furthermore, this is capital that decreases as it is used. This creates a false picture of the real economic situation; that Europe is selling the majority of its assets to the USA, while registering these transactions as increases in turnover. However, raw materials such as oil, gas, and other resources cannot be recycled – they can only be sold once. Once sold, their value cannot be registered again in the accounts, and we can only receive the resultant profit once.

This inborn conflict between the political and legal system on the one hand, and growth and the world of business, on the other, prevents us from creating a new system. Or in simple terms, this slows down the rate of change (or the possibility for change) and time is running out.

Part of the answer lies in the relationship between sustainability and growth. This relationship is absolutely critical. We cannot hope to legislate our way out of crisis. Growth alone, is not the answer. The business world's agenda for profit and growth doesn't take account of the holistic nature of either its cause or effect. Neither is the option to recycle materials and resources considered as a possible competence or asset. Businesses can quite reasonably argue that political governance hasn't demanded this of them, and as such they don't do it. However, businesses that manage to implement a holistic growth strategy, will survive in the long run, for the simple reason that we are, already in our lifetime, running short of vital materials and resources. This is why we can see the emergence of a *circular economy*, or *resource economy*, which links production to consumption-

and subsequent re-use. Perhaps we are beginning to develop our sense for the black swans.

One example of how our resources can be re-used, is the philosophy and concept of *cradle-to-cradle,* created by American architect, William McDonough and German chemist, Michael Braungart. This is a fundamentally new way to design, produce, use and consume. If an office-chair is cradle-to-cradle certified, then all its components can be re-used for a secondary purpose. The construction industry has embraced this idea, and new ways to re-use different resources are already being tested.

Over the past one hundred years, the world's population has grown four times in size. The consumption of biomass has more than tripled and the total use of raw material is eight times greater. The consumption of fossil fuels is twelve times greater, and economic output is twenty-two times greater. If we look at economic output over the last twenty centuries, more than three quarters has been created since 1900, and one quarter since 2000. Today, we use around one third more of our planet than is sustainable.

What will inspire you, as a business leader, to react and change the way you run your business? How could you re-think and incorporate society's long term needs to generate new profit? What will enable your board of directors and your colleagues to change their mindset? Will this be the insight that we cannot regulate ourselves out of crisis, or that there are too few resources to continue our growth strategy ad infinitum? Is it that the silos begin to fall?

Regardless of what it takes for business leaders to change their mindset, the time is now.

Systems should serve us – *Summary*
How, in the future, we can make systems which serve us, instead of sustaining the system we have:
- More detailed legislation means less overview and less responsibility for businesses.
- Less responsibility for businesses means more laws to tell businesses what to do.

- We consider and measure only that which the law describes. In this way, we miss vital information and become unable to see anything new.
- We usually act too late, because we think that there is ample time to implement change.
- To change nothing is not a realistic option since crisis is here to stay.
- Businesses must take responsibility for directing the way forward.
- The building blocks for a new system are freedom, responsibility and an increased ability to reach a balanced and healthy growth strategy, collectively.

INTRO

Meet the bank manager, who turned the logic of banking on its head. 40 years ago! He decentralised the entire business model of Swedish, Handelsbanken with such success that the structure has survived both at home and abroad. Across the water, Handelsbanken will soon become Denmark's largest bank.

Use your Common Sense

"Goodness me, all I did was to use my common sense. And this was all years ago."

In 1970, Dr. Jan Wallander was recruited as the new CEO of Sundsvallsbanken, a regional bank in northern Sweden to help the bank get through crisis. He radically changed the bank's management policies using the common sense thinking he had practiced as a professor in economics. These policies have continued to provide the foundation for the modern Svenska Handelsbanken and for four CEOs since Wallander's exit in 1991. During 1970-1972, Handelsbanken created eight regional banks, each operating with a high degree of independence, to which the branch offices belonged. Much of the decision-making was decentralized to the local and regional level, and the financial management and control system was overhauled by focusing more on reporting and less on central budgeting. The new organisation focused on achieving profitability rather than on volume growth.

When asked how he came to this conclusion, the now 93 year old professor replies:

"My predecessor, who was the head of Sundvallsbanken, like me, lacked practical experience in banking operations. They had had good experience with him. When he left, they were brave enough to offer me the job, despite the fact that I had no knowledge of banking. In fact, they admitted to me that it's actually not too difficult: you just need to use your own common sense. So, I ended up in their director's office, equipped with a booklet on how to work in a bank. I read it as a fresh and naïve student, and should anyone come into the office, I immediately hid it out of sight. The bank had a strong economy, so I had room for error at the time. Because I held a doctorate in philosophy, they assumed that I was very knowledgable. Bit by bit, I began to get the hang of things." Wallander pauses, and then continues, "It was right, what they said. It was just about common sense".

What, in your eyes, is common sense?
"To forget all preconceived ideas on leadership from business schools, books, articles, and American business gurus. Instead sit yourself down and work out what you actually know to be true. Say to yourself: We need to get from A to B, so how do we get there? You need to try out different ways to get there, and then choose one direction, and do it, even if this is the opposite of what everyone else is talking about."

Why aren't there more leaders who are able to do it like this?
"Because they have too many fixed ideas from business school and the media. Get away from this, and think for yourself. At Handelsbanken, we could think for ourselves. We never used consultants. It goes without saying that they need to earn their salary by making changes."

Find the direct way
When Jan Wallander was taken on as CEO of *Handelsbanken* in 1970, he had already instigated a certain stability with regards to his ideas on common sense and decentralization.

You must have had a certain degree of self-confidence to keep hold of this mindset. Would you say that younger business leaders make things unnecessarily hard for themselves?
"Perhaps, yes, perhaps this *is* what I'm saying. Or otherwise I was just affected by my background in academic knowledge. Knowledge, for me, is the simplest thing there is; discovering how different things work and finding the meaning in things without this being pre-assigned. If you end by re-

alising that your solution is opposed to the common opinion of the rest of the world, then this can only be a good thing. I came to banking, and everyday I met hundreds of prescribed opinions on why and how things should be done, just because others did the same. I said, "I'm not interested in that," says Wallander, drawing a large cross in front of himself with his hands. "I want us to sit down together and look at the problem, focusing on how to get from here to there. This is just common sense. It wasn't hard for me, but I am aware that it is for many business leaders."

How did you manage to avoid using organisation diagrams?
"I had begun reading some rather advanced books, which described that banks should have organisation diagrams, and I thought, "Great! This is something I know how to do." But then, one of my colleagues advised me otherwise. If you put people in boxes, it gets difficult to make changes. Subsequent changes in the organisation would then make it all too evident who was moving upwards and who was moving sideways. If you are not bound by this, then changes can occur much more naturally. I tried to see what such a diagram might look like if I did draw it. The result resembled a spider's web, since some people are good at getting contacts, and therefore should be allowed to do this, whilst others are best at something completely different. All the same, to put this on paper would be unnecessarily rigid."

What about job descriptions, and ensuring that people were clear of their responsibilities?
The only important thing to know is who your boss is and, in a bank, who can say yes or no to a loan. Actually, it was clear how much authority each person had in order that they couldn't push decisions higher up in the organisation."

So how did you succeed in creating what some consider to be the most decentralized company in the world?
"Common sense, and common sense," replies Wallander.

What obstacles do you think another company would meet if they attempted to do the same as you did?

"In fact, it took me several years to be conscious of what it was we had done. In essence, this was to decentralize as much as possible and at every step, all the time, push responsibility downwards. Within this process, we kept hearing what a good idea this is, at least as long as you keep being given more responsibility by your boss. When this escalates into power being pushed downwards, things start to go wrong. At this point, we begin to hear objections that those at the bottom don't have sufficient education or perspective, and they don't see the consequences of what they set going. As such, decentralization has a tendency to stop when it has reached a certain level. We used a lot of time and energy over the first three to five years in making the push downwards, saying, "Let's not stop here, you need to keep going, keep delegating downwards." Wallander pushes downwards with the palms of his hands to emphasize the strength which is required. He adds, "This is particularly difficult at the director level. They have worked hard to reach the top of the pyramid, so they don't give away their power so easily, despite agreeing with the effectiveness of the idea. So the great question is, how willing you are, as a leader, to let go of some of your own power."

Did you use your power to take power from yourself?
"Yes."

How was this period?
"Some of the directors felt, with good reason, that this stole their authority. Therefore, they tried to oppose my initiatives by appealing to our board of directors. They created a form of revolution in an attempt to convince the board to replace me. But by this point, we had begun to get so much success that the board didn't listen to them, and it never became much of a problem for me."

A good crisis

When people left the leadership and you needed to find their replacements, what type of people were you after?

"People who could control and relinquish their craving for power. People who would act in the interest of others and not just themselves. Perhaps a slightly more mature kind, one who could be interested in opera," Wallander smiles a dreamy and somewhat childish smile.

Do you think that any kind of business can do what you did?

"Yes, of course. I have also had my difficulties and have spent an inconceivable amount of time trying to persuade people. I was in a good position because, at the time, Handelsbanken was in crisis and was being heavily criticised by the media. The bank was really lost. Then came a man from the outside and said confidently; "You need to do this, and then this."

So timing is important?

"Yes, and a good crisis."

Why did you remove budgets?

"Anyone who has been through business school has learned that budgets are necessary. They have learned the skills and techniques used to create and manage them. But my own experiments in this area lead me to conclude that this was a bad idea. I have been a professor for long-term planning and adviser to the government. The more I learned, the more I could see that things are always in motion, constantly changing. I suspect that the popularity for budgeting came from the budget people themselves who wanted to prove that they were more than just accountants," says Wallander, smiling.

He seems to have found an extra spurt of energy. It was the widespread debate on budgetting which prompted Wallander to write his book *"Budgets – An Unecessary Evil"*. In the book Jan Wallander's reflections on budgeting are serious and comprehensive, but his teasing tone is still unmistakable, "Budgets are a difficult way to reach a conclusion which anyone can clearly see is either right or wrong. In this case budgets can actually become very dangerous in that they can prevent you from adapting to new situations. And, if you don't believe in your budget, there is no point in having one."

HOW HANDELSBANKEN SEES ITSELF AND WALLANDER TODAY

In 1919, Stockholms Handelsbanken merged with the Swedish bank, Bank AB Södra and the name was changed to the Swedish Handelsbanken, or as it is known today, simply, Handelsbanken. In 1969, nearly 100 years after the bank was founded, Handelsbanken ran into deep economic crisis, which resulted in the resignation of the bank's leadership. If the bank were to recover, something drastic needed to happen. It did!

Jan Wallander took the helm as CEO and made clear that he saw everything very differently. From then on, all decisions should be taken as close to the customer as possible and not from centralised departments at HQ. Each branch of the bankwas given full responsibility for their customers, their economy, and their own marketing.

At the same time, central offices were made smaller. Instead of dictating and controlling the tasks of the branches, they began to adopt a support function and act asheir resource-providers. All budgeting was eliminated. Handelsbanken agreed on one goal and two means. The goal was to achieve higher profits than the average profits of the other banks in the home market. The means were more satisfied customers and lower costs than their competitors. As such, Handelsbanken went from having a lower profitability than the other banks in the 1960s, to having equal profitability by 1971, to having surpassed the competition today. Customer satisfaction is the highest in Scandinavia and Handelsbanken is currently the most cost-effective bank in Europe.

Source: www.handelsbanken.dk

NOT ALWAYS AS WE THINK

Two angels on a journey stayed the night at a wealthy family. The family were not hospitable. They didn't allow the angels to sleep in the guest room of the main house. Instead they had to spend the night in a small room in a cold cellar. Whilst they were arranging a place to sleep on the hard floor, the eldest angle notice a hole in the wall and repaired it. When the other angel asked her why she had done so, the eldest angel replied, "Things are not always as we think they are."

The next evening, the two angels stayed with a poor but hospitable farmer's family. After they had all shared the little food that the family had left, the angels were given the double bed so that they could get a good night's sleep. At sunrise the next day, the angels could see that the family were in floods of tears. Their only cow, and their one source of survival, lay dead out in the field. The younger angel was furious and asked the older one, "How could you help the family that was so wealthy but mean and then punish this one, so friendly but poor?"

"Things are not always as we think they are," said the eldest angel. "While we were in the cellar of the wealthy family, I discovered a large sack of gold hidden in the wall. Since the man of the house was so greedy and unwilling to share what he had, then I closed the wall so that he would never find the gold. And whilst we slept at the farm house, I saw the angel of death come to seize the farmer's wife. Therefore I gave the family's cow to the angel of death in place of their wife and mother. Things are not always as we think they are".

– Origin unknown

CHAPTER 3
Across the silos

Things can be very different to the way we think they are. This chapter is about how cooperation creates better solutions than methods of control, which often destroy our sense of community and common feeling. As such, we must find new methods for running business and new economic systems that include the society they operate in. Employees are no longer positioned at the bottom of *the pyramid of needs,* and we need an infrastructure for salary which can fulfill specific aims. The joy and motivation for work is created through cooperation, not alone.

Competition vs. cooperation

The American futurist and social architect, Barbara Marx Hubbard, well-known for her work on evolution, has indicated that we develop via competition but survive via cooperation. Her mantra is clear: Learn to cooperate or die! It is only species that haven't yet learnt to cooperate, that compete with each other. To compete is also a primitive way of being together. It is only when competition is transformed and individuals begin working together that the species can manage to survive. In nature, this happens automatically when the time is right because transformation is a natural part of development. Nature creates new, whole systems out of the parts. In the initial stages of the earth's development, single-cell life was the only kind of life in existence. These single-cells shaped themselves in competition with one another until a transformation occurred and the cells began to cooperate to create the multi-celled life form, the precondition for life as we know it today. Perhaps our current situation is similar: We have come far by competing against each other, but our development cannot continue until we learn to cooperate.

The planet will survive. It has, for billions of years. But if the human race should also survive, then we must adjust and develop our systems and infrastructure to aid us in working together. We need to act collectively and have the ability and will to set our own individual needs aside in order to find common solutions. In the future, the accountancy system which is used for businesses to measure losses and gains must include the vast long-term costs, for example of sourcing non-renewable energy and the environmental pollution that this ensues. Finding common solutions requires a strong entrepreneurial spirit, knowledge, common sense, creativity, and courage. According to Hungarian scientist, musician, and author, Ervin Lazlo: "Knowledge can get us from A to B, whilst fantasy can take us anywhere."

A new helping hand

In the 1950s, John Nash released his mathematical work; *Nash Equilibrium* and *Nash Bargaining for Non-Cooperative Games*. The conclusion was that a group of people who coordinate their work can reach their goal more effectively than an individual who only follows his own aims and needs. Nash's theory can help us to better understand problems, conflicts and partnerships in a range of social, political and economic contexts. An area of research which has made use of Nash's work is game theory. In game theory, one studies the ultimate pathway to choose, when the costs and benefits at each junction depend on the individual choice of others. Professor and Doctor of Politics at the Economic Institute of Copenhagen University, Hans Keiding, explains this as follows: "The company, whose actions are coordinated can reach further, faster, than the company who relies only on uncoordinated individual actions. Game theory can help support such coordinated behaviour by determining how individual actions can be shaped to produce the most cooperative solutions."

In game theory, conflicts and their results are analysed. The form of the conflict is established so that the tests can then explore which results can be explained by different forms of conflict. The structure of the game is described by the number of players, the player options or strategies to make moves and via the game's *payoff*, which focuses on the consequences of the choices available. The theory attempts to answer the question of which strategic choice of those available we can expect the game's players to choose. It is this answer that game theory calls the solution or *equilibrium*.

Since mathematicians von Neumann and Morgenstern put game theory on the agenda, we have made the distinction between *non-cooperative equilibrium*, where players cannot consult each other in the process of decision making, and *cooperative equilibrium*, where consultation and common agreements are permitted. If the game is to run *non-cooperatively*, then the individual player cannot coordinate his strategic choice with others and must instead try to predict what he *expects* others to do. Despite Neumann and Morgenstern dedicating more than half of their book to *non-cooperative* solutions for games, the theory part is less developed due to its complexity. What we do know often concerns specific games covering, for example, negotiation situations, in which a coalition of organised players who can make decisions, face others who cannot. What is most important, in such situations, is how to delegate the potential success of the group to the individual players when the only decision any one player is capable of is to quit the game.

If we want companies to conduct their businesses responsibly, we need to increase transparency and show which companies are actually serving society. This can be done in a variety of ways. For example, customers can award a star-rating similar to the *"smiley"* system used for Danish restaurants. In this case, The Danish Ministry of Health gives points according to an index, based on parameters such as hygiene. These points add up to a total result which is communicated publicly with a sad or smiley icon depending on how the restaurant performed in the test. By creating transparency amongst companies who benefit society, it becomes possible to use cooperation as a means of staying competitive. The companies who are best at cooperating will survive in the long run, since they will be the ones remembered and rewarded by society. A recent example is OECD and G8's intention to increase the transparency of multinational companies with respect to the tax they pay. In days gone by, those who didn't contribute to the collective were locked into a pillory in the town's most public square. The pillory has rightly been abolished, but the principle of public display is still valid. A company who doesn't serve the whole system can in this way be exposed publicly and, as such, be obliged to take responsibility for their actions.

An up to date and more humane version of the pillory is the Danish Institute for Mediation and Complaints (MKI) initiative to promote corporate responsibility. MKI works towards ensuring that business activities that are damaging to society cannot be allowed to yield profit. The aim of MKI is to expose cases in which a company has not complied with OECD's requirements for multinational corporate responsibility. This can concern human or labour rights, or negative impact on climate or the environment. The aim of OECD's standards is to make it mandatory for companies to contribute to economic, social, and environmental prosperity whilst minimising all negative impacts. MKT strives to create a forum for mediation, dialogue, and the resolution of conflict. Those cases which most seriously violate the standards are published on MKI's website according to a *name and shame*" principle which, in effect, is a contemporary form of the pillory.

Control (in danish *Kontrol*) spelt backwards (= *Lort nok)* = Enough crap!

No one wants to be controlled or repeatedly told what they are doing wrong! A culture which focuses on error and control is built on the mindset that the person or component which caused the error can and should be identified. This results in everyone looking for a scapegoat. Such a company culture obstructs the possibility for a holistic perspective of the company. Collective spirit cannot grow in a company with this kind of zero-error mentality. This will only create individual competition, both among those being controlled and those doing the controlling. For the latter group, conflicts arise as people dodge responsibility in order to avoid the risk of making mistakes.

It is common for medical companies to have a *quality control* (QC) function to make sure that their production adheres to the rules of *good manufacturing practice* (GMP). The people responsible for the production line often feel criticised by those working in the QC function when they point to "errors" in the way people have carried out their jobs. This can lead to employees taking sides in opposition to each other. Such polarisation between different departments doesn't mean that individual people don't like each other, more that people don't like to be criticised and told that they are doing things wrong. The conflict is not interpersonal but structural, and it is a fault of the system. This problem can be solved systematically by finding alternative ways to support and facilitate production.

Before industrialisation, there were more generalists in the workplace. Single personnel had the overview of many work lines at once and were present throughout the process, from first idea to finished product. This made sense for everyone and it gave those involved a clear understanding of why production was dealt with in the way it was. Now, we have organised a labour market in such a way that very few are involved with the entire process. Some people come up with the idea, whilst others implement it, regardless of whether they understand it or not, agree or disagree with it, or believe or don't believe that it will work in practice. The fundamental human need to connect brain and hand is no longer fulfilled. Some are assigned to sit at desks and generate big ideas, but without being allowed to implement these ideas with their own hands. Others are assigned to the manual or technical tasks of implementing the idea without understanding the thinking behind it. This isolates us in silos and we all lose meaning in what we are working with, for, and towards.

The control function was introduced at the same time as the specialist came into the picture. When a team of, for example, ten men assembles a car and each is given a separate task, quality control from the central office is a necessary part of guaranteeing the functionality of the product. The control function is there to shed light on any defects or deficiencies. When the controller comes on the scene, it is often too late to make corrections because the product is finished and the error has been made. In this way, a system is created in which no one wins. The controller then focuses on errors occurring at the boundary or bridge between silos and the typical reaction is to introduce new controls early on in the process. As described in Chapter Two, this creates an endless cycle of new legislation being introduced in an attempt to fill gaps between that which already exists.

When the controller success criteria is to finecomb all mistakes under the names of *quality control, quality assurance* and *audit*, it is easy for mistrust to become embedded in the organisation. The employees feel that they are at an exam whenever the controller comes around, and all that matters is to *pass*. Mistrust for the production side kicks in on the side of the controllers if they discover anyone on the shop floor covering up their mistakes. When this happens, instead of concentrating on finding the solution which works out best for everyone, as soon as the controller has exposed the error, people start to defend the work they have done and push the blame to employees in another silo. Often this isn't done vindictively, but is due to a lack of knowledge or understanding with regards to what is actually going on in the other silos.

Thirty years ago, the CEO of Swedish *Handelsbanken*, made a controversial decision to abolish the controller function (see the interview with Wallander from page 43). This function was not increasing the value of the organisation and was not meeting people's social needs or their need for recognition. People don't want others to find mistakes in what they are doing. When we are prey to criticism, this does not increase our motivation or will to go the extra mile. On the contrary, we fall back into a defensive position and use more energy in holding up our shield than in working openly and constructively towards finding a solution. Jan Wallander knew well that control (in Danish *kontrol*) spelt backwards is *"lort nok"* meaning "enough crap," and that control was not the way of creating a business culture where everyone is ready to take responsibility for reaching the best solution. He knew that one of the most important *drivers* for people and employees is our need for recognition and respect.

Wallander was met with skepticism from his leadership when he closed down this wellestablished controller function. He had gained the courage for making big decisions during his time as a researcher when he had taught himself to see things soberly and objectively. If things didn't make sense and didn't bring anything positive to the organisation, then no reason to have them. In his book *"Med den manskliga naturen – inte mot!"* *("With the Human Nature - not against!"),* he describes how vital it is to have an indepth knowledge of what drives people and which needs people want to be fulfilled. Since criticism has a negative effect on human nature, why retain a position that criticises people and finds mistakes?

Handelsbanken could only remove their controller function because they pulled down their silos. The bank went from being a centralised organisation with a high degree of specialisation (and with it, a long list of top-down instructions) to being a company run by local responsibility. The bank became decentralised. Each local branch was given total responsibility for their customers since they were closest to them and best at establishing their respective needs.

Wallander saw the commercial advantage in not spending valuable time finding errors, and created an entirely different business culture to the competitors. The other banks

**"What is the most basic thing in leadership?"
asked the journalist. "When I replied 'love', he
fell silent, but this is precisely what I consider the
answer to be."**

- Ingvar Kamprad, IKEA's founder and owner in the book:
"Kamprad's lilla gulblå" (Kamprad's little yellow-blue)

stuck to existing and outdated theories of economics and
leadership, from a time when employees had very different
needs and expectations than today, when their top priorities were the comfort and security that came from following precise orders and being told exactly what was right and
wrong. At this time, command and control systems could
fulfill the employees' desire for clear instructions and for a
strong leader who could check that the tasks within each silo
were being carried out correctly.

Employees in the West have developed since this bygone
era. Nowadays, they want other things than comfort. Freedom,
for example, carries high value. Popular human demand is
moving away from small specialised units, and towards holistic systems. When employees desire the freedom to think for
themselves and when they are able to see how the parts make
up the whole, the entire system needs to built differently.

Wallander used his common sense to ask the question no
one else asked: Why should there be a controller function
at all? Why, instead, couldn't they all fulfil this job uncon-
sciously. This not only avoided the company paying heavy
salaries, but enabled people to think freely and take responsibility for themselves. *Common sense* is an important tool to
help us argue against the structures that no longer work for
us. This is about questioning everything and taking nothing
for granted. Do you, for example, know why train tracks are
spaced at the width they are from each other? This width
corresponds to the distance between the two hind legs of
the horse which pulled the wagons. The Romans had built
so many bridges that when building the rail lines, we wanted
the trains to be able to use the same bridges.

Employees want trust, respect and development

Let us dig deeper into established behavioural and motivational theory in order to test the hypothesis that many companies still lead their employees in a way that attempts to fulfill a set of needs that have gradually lost importance and been replaced by others.

According to Maslow, people's needs should be considered holistically. In his book, *Motivation and Personality* from 1954, Maslow describes his motivational theory for explaining which factors are instrumental in causing us to act in a particular way. There is always an original need behind any action, interest, wish, or demand. These needs are seen as being the reason for us feeling the way we feel. If our needs are fulfilled, then we feel happy. If our needs are not fulfilled then we become sad or angry. These human needs are represented in figure 2 on page 62. The two needs at the top of the pyramid are the needs for recognition and self-realisation, or self-actualization as Maslow chose to call it. These are growth needs, and it is with these that we have our greatest chance to develop.

When creating the organisation for *Handelsbanken*, Jan Wallander allowed his priorities to be influenced by the Maslow pyramid. He wanted to know what really drove people. Which processes and structures should be retained, which should be replaced and what kind of new ones should be implemented. By considering human nature and the needs that drive us, it was much easier for Wallander to construct a new structure and remove all unnecessary routines, processes, and structures, that didn't serve human needs. On the following pages, you can read more about our needs and see how different companies have tried to satisfy them in the past. Very few companies have, as yet, succeeded in meeting the employees' needs for self-actualisation.

continues on page 65

The needs on one level must be fulfilled, before moving up to the next level.

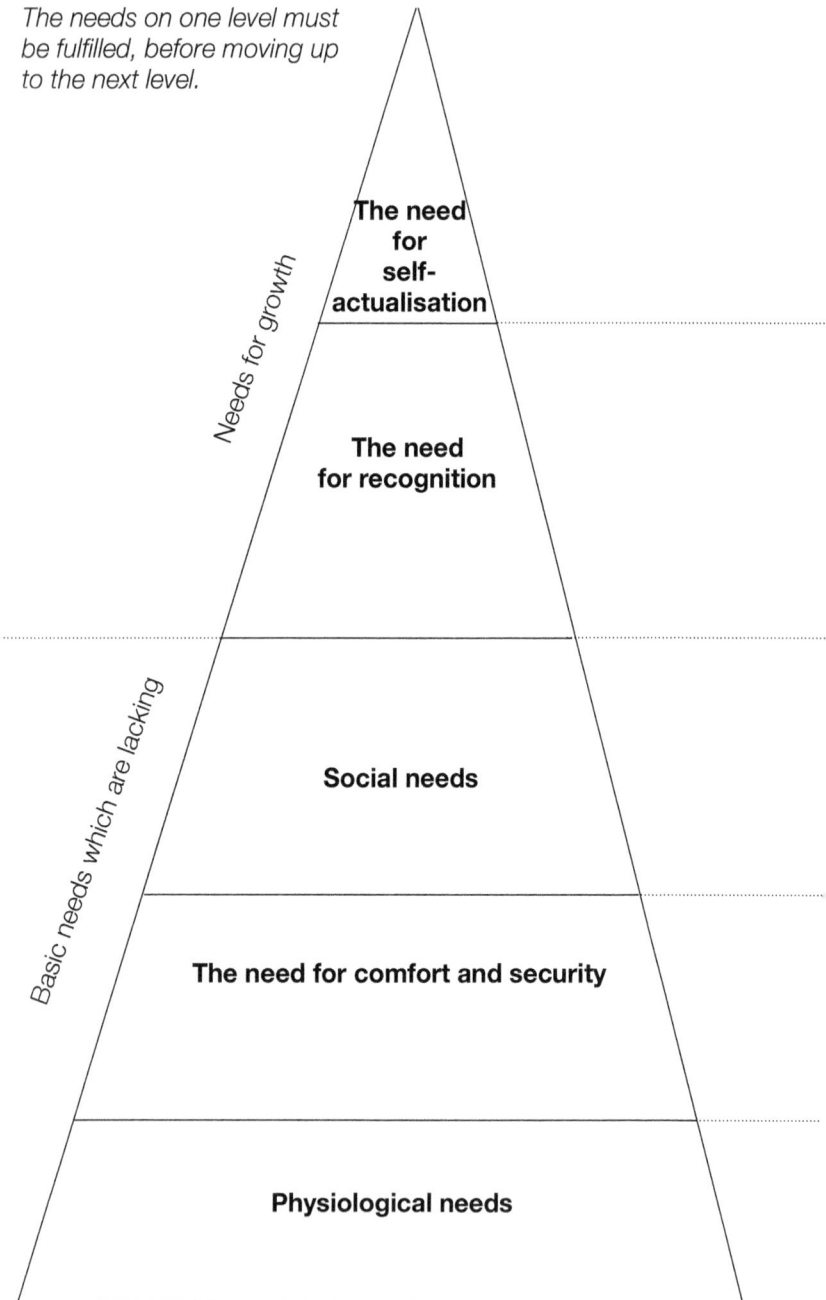

The need for self-actualisation

The need for recognition

Social needs

The need for comfort and security

Physiological needs

Needs for growth

Basic needs which are lacking

The need for self-actualisation

People reaching this fifth and final level have had all basic needs fulfilled. As such, they accept themselves, are self-sufficient, democratic, flexible, and are ready to realise each new opportunity using their specific competences. People at this level seek new experiences and challenges and bring others with them along the way. They have a holistic overview, a wider perspective and work towards making things connected and cohesive. They want to feel meaning in what they do and experience a collective spirit. They want to be part of companies which allow employees to contribute to more than the company's bottom line.

The need for recognition

The fourth level covers values such as self-respect, confidence, knowledge, status and receiving respect from others. People need to feel that they are seen, heard and valued. This need for recognition and respect comes into play once physiological needs and the needs for comfort and security have been fulfilled. The need for employees to be treated with decency and re-spect has lead to companies introducing "employee development meet-ings" to allow an open and honest dialogue with regards to where people see themselves relative to the company and their own career.

Social needs

The third level covers needs for community, love and friendship. Companies have attempted to meet these needs with parties, employee events, clubs and unions. The Human Resource facility (HR) was introduced here, as an important part of the company. Laws and regulations were introduced to set standards for one's psychological perception of their work environment and in order to prevent personal harassment.

The need for comfort and security

The second level covers emotional needs and needs relating to personal comfort; safety, security, stability, order, and protection against fear. In the middle of the 1900s, regulation to improve the quality of the work environ-ment and aspects of safety became paramount for industrial workers.

Physiological needs

The first level holds all basic needs; for food, water, air, sleep and for protec-tion from wind, rain and cold. If these needs are not met then this condition will dominate people's behaviour and consciousness. In the beginning of the 1900s, it was these physiological needs plus the need to set a minimum wage which were most important for industrial workers.

CREATIVE CAPITALISIM - THE TEN COMMANDMENTS

Michael Kinsley, editor of the book *"Creative Capitalism"*, in which Bill Gates is one of the main contributors, summarises as follows:

1. Today's miracles of technology benefit only those who can afford them. Markets respond only to "demand", not to "need".

2. This is a systemic flaw in the free-market system. Further technological innovation is less important than systemic innovation to mend this flaw.

3. The world is getting better, but not fast enough and not in a way which is inclusive for all. Great advances in technology therefore make inequity worse. About a million people are left out. For example, climate change will impose the worst effects on those least responsible for it.

4. Why? Because in "a system of pure capitalism", the incentive to serve people rises as their wealth rises and falls as their wealth falls. This system needs to be changed so that there is incentive to serve poor people too.

5. Self-interest is just one of two forces in human nature. The other is "caring for others." The genius of capitalism is that it makes self-interest serve the general interest. Philanthropy and government are supposed to address our "caring for others," but there isn't enough philanthropic or government money to solve the world's problems.

6. A revised capitalist system would both make a profit and improve the lives of the have-nots.

7. A revised system should use profit incentives where possible. But even where profits are not possible, there is a market-based incentive that can be used: recognition. Positive recognition is good for a company's reputation, good for attracting customers, and good for attracting employees.

8. Creative capitalism is a system where incentives for both profit and recognition motivate both self-interest and caring for others.

9. Under creative capitalism, governments, businesses, and non-profits work together.

10. "This hybrid engine of self-interest and concern for others serves a much wider circle of people than can be reached by self-interest or caring alone."

Production or love

Niels Stokholm, who was due to become professor at Denmark's Technical University (DTU), chose the practical route instead of research. He was born in South Jutland, educated as a civil engineer, and then emigrated to Canada to build bridges. At the age of 42, he was offered a professorship at DTU, which he declined because in his opinion the world was more in need of a biodynamic farmer than another bridge. Today, he runs a biodynamic farm in the north of Zealand and holds Denmark's last herd of red milking cows. Niels holds many lectures on biodynamic agriculture at different venues around the world. At one of these, he was asked how many litres he produces in one year. His answer was "None at all!" The person who asked the question looked surprised, and asked again, "But you must produce some with all those milk cows you have!" Niels answered, "I don't produce milk, I *cultivate* milk."

Perhaps you are smiling a little at this, because what difference does it make whether milk is "produced" or "cultivated"? The result is the same. Or is it? If we "produce", then this is all about the result. If, on the other hand, we "cultivate" this is about *why* we do what we do. It's about our passion, since this is what gives meaning to it all. Only by being conscious of our *why*, are we able to keep an overview, and when we have this we can discover what we need to do and how to do it.

When we are driven by our need for meaning, recognition, and respect, we can create something we can be proud of. We have no desire to be measured mechanically on how much we can produce. A process driven by meaning and enjoyment will run a lot more smoothly than one driven by whip or carrot. The number of people working voluntarily has risen dramatically in recent years with Denmark, Sweden, and Holland, holding the highest concentrations in Europe. If the same motivation that arises from doing something meaningful - from cultivating something - could be applied to business, then both the level of happiness and profit could rise. When we work together we receive pay back in the form of a happiness and trust hormone called oxytocin. This is referred to as the hug hormone, since it is released with an embrace lasting more than thirty seconds.

IKEA's founder and owner, Ingvar Kamprad, has always practised leadership through his touch and by showing is love for people. In larger gatherings, he can give hugs to up to a thousand people as he greets them. In other words, Kamprad cultivates his business.

Creative capitalism

Microsoft's founder Bill Gates is one of the richest people on earth. He has built one of the largest companies in the world from scratch. Many consider him to be the perfect prototype capitalist. So why mention Gates when we are otherwise occupied with businesses which are creating their own road maps and carving alternative paths in our present capitalist system?

In 2008, Bill Gates appeared in Time Magazine with this call to us all:

Capitalism has improved the quality of life for billions of people; something that is easy to forget in a time of serious economic uncertainty, but it has also excluded billions of people. These people have large scale and urgent needs, but they have not expressed these needs in a way the market can react to. They are stuck in poverty, they suffer from diseases that could be prevented and they have never had the chance to make something of their lives. Governments and NGOs have a critical task in helping them, but it will take too long for them to do this alone. There are companies who do have the know how to create technological innovations that can help those in poverty. In order to get the most out of these resources, we need a creative capitalism that can increase the orbit of the market forces. We need new ways to bring many more people into the system that has created so much good in the world.

In other words, Bill Gates is searching for a new form of capitalism. It should be designed so that the incentives of the market in terms of profit and recognition can also be available to the poor. Bill Gates made a similar plea to serve society as well as money in his keynote speech at Davos in 2008. He exposed himself to ridicule and received criticism from, amongst others, the influential judge and economist Richard Posner, for contradicting the traditional definition of capitalism, in which the primary focus is to generate profit. The fact that Bill Gates stands up to say that what we are doing is no longer working, and that we should find an alternative, has, in itself, had the effect that his opponents have begun listening.

According to the Edelman Trust Barometer 2012, the world's population, at that time, had more faith in business leaders than in politicians. This is consistent with the premise that businesses can make the difference that governments cannot make alone. Most people tend to agree that businesses do have a social responsibility and as such, have a duty to look beyond their own silo. But, at the same time, *corporate social responsibility* (CSR) has become an integrated part of silo-thinking in many large companies. Initiatives are often run from fragmented silos instead of being an integral part of the core business and overall mindset of the company. In this way, CSR becomes more a question of which competences or behaviour one individual silo can demonstrate, rather than what the company, as a whole, *could* do if a social responsibility strategy was launched across silos and with each one offering its support. This kind of CSR strategy, drawn as a core reason for the company to exist, would have a lot more meaning for the employees, and make them more inclined to support a successful outcome.

This demands that the leader can follow new directions. John Mackey, who isn't as well known in Scandinavia as Bill Gates, launched his first organic supermarket in 1978. Later, this became the Whole Foods Market which, for the twelfth year in a row, has been named by Fortune Magazine as one of the top one hundred best companies to work for in the USA. In 2011, Whole Foods Market had 60,000 employees alone in the USA, a turnover of 1.2 billion dollars and a profit of 342 million dollars. When John Mackey started the company, he approached a venture fund in search of capital. He was rejected, being told that they weren't going to fund a company that sold "hippie food to hippies." Several years later, after Whole Foods Market had become a huge success, Mackey met the director of the venture fund who had been so outspoken. He admitted to Mackey that he had made the mistake of his life in not investing in the company.

The Whole Foods Market values are: to sell natural and organic products of the highest possible quality; to satisfy and please their customers; to make sure that their employees are able and happy; to create welfare through profit and growth; to take good care of our society and environment; to strike long-term, win-win partnerships with suppliers; and to promote the health of stakeholders via education and good diet. The company has taken on a responsibility for society that reaches far beyond the thick walls of the silo. Since the values are expressed by the employees and the company is transparent, then it is rewarded with consumers.

Conscious capitalism

Like Bill Gates, John Mackey possesses significant surplus, both with regards to his wealth and his will to do something to help. Because of this, he has decided to put forth the business model he calls *Conscious Capitalism*. He believes that this model can solve the problems which our existing system suffers from, in that it allows us both to make money and do good. In order for the world of business to reach its full potential in the 21st Century, according to Mackey, we need to create a new business paradigm that can encompass complex systems which are intertwined and mutually dependent. This requires a departure from rigidity and closed ended systems and an entry into integrated and holistic systems. There are two preconditions which must be in place for a company to practise *Conscious Capitalism:* first, it must be based on a stakeholder model, and second it must be driven by passion and meaning.

Mackey believes that we need to redefine who and what is most important for the company. It is not only investors, customers and employees who are the stakeholders, but also the company's suppliers and the communities surrounding all operations.

A company's most important aim cannot only be to generate profit. Passion and meaning are necessary ingredients within any business environment. This has the effect of creating motivation and enjoyment for the employees. People need to be able to contribute positively to the greater good, and understand the overall meaning in what they do. People have progressively worked themselves upwards in Maslow's pyramid and now is the time for companies to do the same. Mackey tells us that the way to happiness cannot be found in hunting happiness, but by doing something that has meaning. The same applies to profit. The way to profit cannot be found in hunting profit, but by doing something which has meaning and contributes something of value to others. If one finds this, one will also begin earning money.

In order to find passion, meaning, and direction in and for their business, companies can learn a lot from Plato's timeless insights with regards to *the good, the true and the beautiful*. Within these insights lies the discovery of what can work to serve the whole. This becomes the most natural way and the most natural choice and is far removed from striving to achieve maximum performance from each individual element. John Mackey adds to this, by making a call for the *heroic*.

Thus, we have a guiding framework for all companies who want to commit to a higher purpose than only generating profit. But is this at all possible in a silo? Well, no, because it means that people must be able to take responsibility for their *own* actions and be in a position to collaborate across silos to reach the best solution. Unfortunately, this still rarely happens.

We get what we measure. Or, as Professor Steen Hildebrandt of Copenhagen Business School quotes Einstein, *"Not everything that can be measured counts, and not everything that counts can be measured."* In a sustainable paradigm, we measure success and failure in more dimensions than just profit on the bottom line. In an article in the New York Times from September 22nd 2009, we can read how Nobel prize winning economist, Joseph Stiglitz together with Amartya Sen, recommends a new measuring system which takes into account human welfare aswell as economic wealth. In their eyes, much of the cause behind the 2008 economic crisis can be attributed to politicians believing that growth can bring profit to everyone. Stiglitz remarks that,*"What you measure, affects what you do. If you don't measure the right thing, you won't do the right thing".*

When a company puts its focus on profit, then neither the well being of its employees or society will be seen as key priorities, since they become means rather than ends. But what if they become ends in themselves? Bhutan, in the Himalayan mountains, has begun to place well being and happiness as national end goals. As such, Bhutan has started to measure the level of *Gross National Happiness (GNH)* instead of only Gross National Product (GNP). Parameters for measuring this happiness are based on sustainable development, the preservation and promotion of cultural values, the conservation of the natural environment, and the establishment of good governance. Bhutan has already inspired France, Canada and the UK to measure the state of well being within their own countries. Canada's *Index of Well Being* measures levels of poverty and capital along with factors of health, ecology, education, culture, and *work-life balance*. We can decide for ourselves which parameters to include, when we begin measuring our companies' and our country's ability to be good, true, beautiful and heroic.

Let us all swim in the blue ocean

In 2005, W. Chan Kim and Renée Mauborgne of the French business school, INSEAD, published their book, Blue Ocean Strategy. In this book, they unfurl a new business strategy where the focus is shifted from being fastest, cheapest and best, to discovering a business idea so unique that the competition doesn't even enter the game. An example of just such a unique idea is Cirque de Soleil, the biggest live entertainment company in the world. Their highly individual and original combination of circus, music, show and art has reached such synergy that no other competitor, as yet, exists. What Cirque de Soleil have done can also be described as *emergence*. When we see them perform, we experience live how the whole adds up to much more than the sum of the parts. This is largely due to the cooperative relationship which the people involved have managed to create between the different artistic disciplines. All this is covered in more detail later on in this book.

Another example, where we can sense more characteristics in the finished experience than from multiple single ingredients or any lesser combination, is the Danish restaurant, Noma. Named as the top restaurant in the world in 2012, Noma has consistently managed to stay fully booked and charge high prices, even throughout the economic crisis. Noma's *blue ocean strategy* is to use Nordic raw ingredients to create a unique experience of both food and culture. In Noma's own words their strategy is *"to revitalise the Nordic kitchen by embracing the North Atlantic region and providing light to the world through good taste and regional specificity."*

A *blue ocean strategy* can be the strategy that brings us out of the silos by making us think differently and creatively and allowing us to leave older, more rigid and more controlled systems behind. A *blue ocean strategy* is built on a synergetic mindset, in which the elements are configured in a new way in order to create an entirely new product. To achieve this, we should first bid farewell to the silos and construct new platforms. An environment to support cross-platform cooperation can be created by synergies struck between colleagues, ideas and products. This will afford people enjoyment in their work, give meaning to their efforts and generate an increase base line profit.

The Danish futurist Rolf Jensen once said that if Danish companies could conceptualise their ability to work together and if they could write this on the back of a postage stamp, this would be of higher export value than all Denmark's pigs and windmills combined. Director of the Technological Institute, Jane Wickmann, tells of Americans coming to Denmark to be inspired by the Scandinavian model and how the Vice-President of Singapore came specifically to see and learn how people work together and what it takes to create such a model. The problem is that the Danes are not yet able to precisely explain or express what it is they do, let alone write it down on the back of a stamp so that everyone else gets it.

People enquired about the Nordic model at Davos in 2011. This prompted the Council of Nordic Ministries to write and publish the report, "The Nordic Way". The report underlined the particular trust and respect that Nordic people feel towards each other. Furthermore, it described people's general trust in public institutions. A culture like this yields fruit in times of crisis as people flock together to support the group rather than just themselves. As such, we, the Danes, can function as agile rubber dinghies as opposed to rigid super tankers.

Cutting across silos – *Summary*

- Business leaders are often better positioned to solve global problems than politicians, since people tend to have more faith in them, and business is usually closer to the problems.
- Specialisation and detailed processing makes the controller function a necessity. This function preempts opposition from those who are being controlled and can lead to the company becoming fragmented.
- Companies measure an individual or single silo's return in terms of the resulting benefit to the silo and not as a cost or benefit to the company, its environment and its people as a whole, since this extends beyond the current scope of corporate social responsibility.
- We lead people as if they were at the bottom of Maslow's pyramid of needs (fig 2, page 62). In reality, people are often towards the top of the pyramid where they expect to be able to understand and influence the bigger picture.
- Our current capitalist model should develop in a more conscious and creative direction so that we consider more dimensions in our daily work than only economy.
- We need to think between and across silos by establishing synergetic relationships, promoting emergence and putting the pieces together differently.
- If the Nordic countries could conceptualise their own business model and unique design for cooperation, then this would give a high value product for global export.

Part II: BUILD THE PLATFORMS

"We are vigilant with our relationships,
mindful to counteract the polarizing dynamics of this time".
– *Margaret Wheatley*

"Nature creates whole new systems out of separate parts."
– *Barbara Marx Hubbard*

NEW BRAIN SPACE

Legend has it that when Columbus' ship arrived in America, the Indians didn't notice the ship. In all the time the Indians had been there, they had never seen an object out in the water. They hadn't developed the brain space to receive information on the ship's existence. The Shaman, however, noticed a small change in the water's surface which kept him staring at the very position where the ship was at. After some time, the Shaman could begin to decipher the ship's mast and afterwards its sail and hull. He turned to his people and began to explain the separate elements that he saw. Since the Indians trusted their Shaman, then they believed what he described and by the end they too could see the ship.

– Ancient legend

CHAPTER 4

Elements for the new platforms

Just like the Indians that saw a ship for the first time, today's companies need to realise that the individual elements which are emerging on the horizon will one day come together to create a new system to replace the silos. We must build platforms that are flexible and which allow us to work together towards a higher purpose. The platforms should be built based on the three elements of growth, integration, and sustainability. In this chapter, you can gain useful methods and tools for establishing new platforms in and for your company. You will hear from visionary business leaders and organisations, and learn how to set superordinate goals, and create motivation, satisfaction and cooperation.

What comes after the silos?

Our present silo-model is no longer working for us and the three crises of economy, energy, and the environment are all symptoms which demonstrate that our fragmented, short-term system is out of sync with our needs as individuals, as companies, and as a society. A business leader once said to me during a seminar, "It's all well and good that we should demolish the silos, but even more interesting is what comes afterwards."

In Chapter Three, we dealt with the base elements required for constructing the new platforms. By platform, I mean an adaptable structure that accommodates enough space for finding, connecting, and supporting those who want to work towards the same objective. In the Star Wars prequel, The Phantom Menace, each member of parliament, standing within their own cell, represents a particular standpoint or piece of knowledge. When a member from one cell wants to work together with another, then the cells move towards each other, in towards the centre. When the dialogue is over and its purpose fulfilled, the cells withdraw to their position in the outer circle.

To achieve such a dynamic platform, we must work with three key elements: First, *growth*, which gives flow, second, *integration*, which gives mutuality, and third, *sustainability*, which creates balance. I will return to these elements in the next chapters and, in particular, in the third section of the book.

Cooperation is essential when working on a platform, but at the moment, we are not as well-practised in this as we are in competing against each other. We have learnt to compete in order to be fastest, best, and cheapest, but we haven't dedicated the same amount of energy in creating the conceptual basis for making separate units function together as a whole. Here, I can imagine that the waters will part at some point and it will become evident which businesses will survive and which won't. The ones that haven't learned to cooperate will struggle to survive. However, in my work as a mediator, I meet a lot of business leaders who don't believe that it is possible to engage in win-win partnerships and still come out with a profit. A typical question is: "Do you really believe in all you tell us about *win-win*, that we can simply make the cake bigger and make greater profit by supporting each other? We know too well that if a bag of money is lying on the floor and the lights go out, everyone will fight to grab the most money for themselves."

Our doubt and lack of trust stems from our uncertainty in whether the others will be generous towards the group or whether they will think only of themselves in order to sub-optimise their silo and base-line economy. We doubt that others consider themselves and their actions as being part of a bigger, more holistic picture.

In the West today, we are not as trusting as those Indians who believe in their Shaman when he tells them that there is a ship out at sea, without having to see it for themselves. We

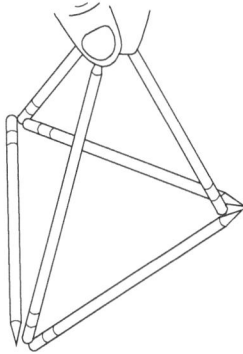

How the sum is greater than the individual elements, or how 1 + 1 = 4

are much more reserved when faced with the uncertainty of change. But when we realise what we are missing out on by not believing in a better future, then our desire to be a part of it increases.

Economic game theory shows that we can reach a better result through cooperation, and instinctively we know this to be the case. In general, when we work together we can achieve more than we could have achieved on our own. Another way to look at it is; 1 + 1 = 4.

Imagine that you are in one silo and your colleague is in another. You are both given three pencils of equal length and are asked how many equilateral triangles you can make. The answer is of course that you can make one each. But if we pull down your silos and set you exactly the same task, what is the answer now? When you are allowed to work together then you won't only make two separate triangles but four by raising the first triangle into a pyramid with four sides (see fig. 3).

We see a synergy effect occurring as the edge of one triangle simultaneously acts as the edge for the next. The end result (in this case, the number of triangles) gets bigger when we are able and willing to pool all our resources. As a team, we solved the problem in *three* dimensions as opposed to two.

It's easy enough to tell people that they need to trust one another and work together, but, in practice, this proves difficult if we are not in complete agreement with respect to the objectives or success criteria. Many companies have problems with bonus schemes which result in employees not wanting to cooperate. This can happen when, for example, different employees are measured against different performance criteria and begin to compete. In the single silo, an attempt is often made to solve this problem by fine combing the bonus scheme and adjusting the performance criteria. But in fact, the problem can get worse the more the leadership delves into details. The solution is easier to find when we see things from a wider perspective. This reveals the bigger picture and can help us to find a common direction that everyone can understand. In order to enable us to work together in a company, we need a clear and common goal for what we are doing and a sound framework within which to work.

Social psychology looks at how people's thoughts, feelings, and behaviour are influenced by the actual, imagined or preconceived actions of others. The father of social psychology, Muzafer Sherif, PhD wrote the book, *The Robber's Cave Experiment,* in 1961. This book covers an experiment which challenges two competing groups to work together. The experiment took place in 1950s at the University of Oklahoma with 24 twelve-year old boys from middle-class protestant backgrounds. They were divided into two teams, *The Eagles and The Rattlers,* and made to compete in activities such as *"tug of war"* with each team at the end of a thick rope, trying to pull the other team towards them. The two teams of boys quickly became protective and power minded. They began attacking the others' camp at night. Individual identities were defined according to which group a boy belonged to, and differences in character were made stronger and clearer. There was no trust between one group and the other, and they considered themselves enemies. The psychologists carrying out the experiment attempted to bring the boys together by letting them meet on neutral ground. They took them on trips to the beach together, they saw a film with them and even held a common party but this wasn't enough to remove the opposition, mistrust and hate that had been created between them. They made no contact with the other team at these common events. They kept strictly within their own teams.

Superordinate goals draw people together

If we apply the lessons from this experiment to the transition from silos to platforms, it is not enough that we attempt to remove the silos by physically placing people in open offices. The problems arising from the silos will still be present. The harmful competition between groups, departments, and individuals, doesn't disappear just because we take the walls away. The experiment with the teams of boys can help us to understand how we can replace silos with platforms. The researchers tried another strategy when the meetings on neutral ground proved ineffective. They introduced so-called *superordinate goals* as a set of common objectives. These goals caused relations between the boys to change for the better, because they were obliged to work together for the goal to be accomplished. Examples included bringing water to the camp, or setting their bus free from the mud. A *superordinate goal* needs to be big enough and convincing enough for individuals and groups to overcome their personal differences in order to accomplish something important which would otherwise be beyond their reach.

The first pictures taken of earth from space made all those who saw them conscious that we share the same planet. In the same way, we can create an aerial picture of our silos from above by using *superordinate goals* and then use these to remove the silos. Companies which are divided into silos create opposition by agreeing on a common enemy outside the company, but a company made of platforms finds a superordinate goal within the company to join everyone in agreement. A superordinate goal creates a common direction for all. Both leadership and employees alike begin

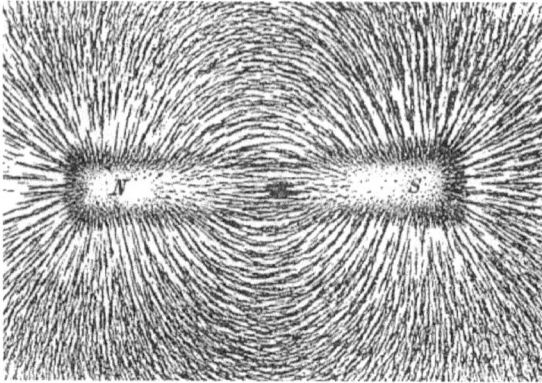

A superordinate goal attracts employees and creates forces of attraction like a magnet which is put on a piece of paper full of iron filings. The picture shows the lines of attraction caused by the magnetic force. Magnet from Practical Physics, publ. 1914 by Macmillan and Company.

serving an objective and a common good that is bigger than themselves as individuals - 1 + 1 = 4, as the example with the pencils demonstrates. A platform is an elastic structure which allows enough space and tolerance for all its resources to come forward, supporting all those who share the same objective for achieving a specific result.

An example of how two elements become attracted to a *common goal* can be illustrated by placing a magnet on a sheet of paper full of iron filings (see fig. 4). In this case, the magnet is the *common goal* which organises the existing magnetism in the iron filings by forcing them to settle on their lines of attraction. The forces are not created from nothing; they are already present within the materials. The same applies for the higher purpose of a company in that the potential for attraction is already present within each employee, and therefore creates a pull effect.

If a company can find, activate, connect, and support what is already present in its people, it can save a great deal of resources by, for example, avoiding having to create and

> **"Classic economic theory, based as it is on an inadequate theory of human motivation, could be revolutionized by accepting the reality of higher human needs, including the impulse to self actualization and the love for the highest values."**
>
> *– Abraham Maslow*

sustain silo structures. The majority of positive initiatives led by companies are operated by human resources (HR) or corporate social responsibility departments (CSR). As departments, they risk being encapsulated in the existing system and traditional structures because this is how we have always organised things. But neither HR, CSR or any other cross-disciplinary focus area can be effectively placed in isolated departments. Instead, they must be integrated in core business and follow their superordinate in order for the company to survive long term.

There are two preconditions for creating a superordinate goal or higher purpose. Both of these must be present before the leadership and employees can be mobilised: first, everyone needs to agree on the goal, and for this to happen everyone must find it appealing and see the meaning in it; and second, the purpose can only be fulfilled if everyone co-operates, and this means that all resources must be present and available.

Everyone must understand that the goal is only reached by everyone contributing. The superordinate goal used by the psychologists as a "magnet" in their experiment with the teams of boys, was to arrange that there wasn't enough drinking water left in the camp. The boys needed to cooperate in order to solve a problem which was essential for their day-to-day survival. Together, they found a water tank in which a sack of sand had got stuck such that the water couldn't run freely. Everyone contributed to fixing the problem and everyone was willing to support each other and the superordinate goal.

An example of a globally higher purpose is the removal of apartheid in South Africa. The film, *"Invictus"* relates how Nelson Mandela, in spite of his skeptics, dedicated his time and efforts in convincing people to supporting a superordinate goal for the South African rugby team to win the World Cup. The plan succeeded, and the fact that everyone supported the same team is considered as an instrumental factor in unifying the country.

When a company finds a superordinate goal which all employees can support, then a synergy and common feeling is created which resembles the lines of force that the iron filings made around the magnet. The Danish company NOVO Nordisk has a superordinate goal to cure diabetes. The goal is attractive for all and it can only be reached if every employee plays their part (read the interview on page 173). The telecom company, *CallMe,* has the superordinate goal of creating a "talk nicely" culture and therefore unsubscribes its customers when they don't talk nicely. In the interviews we have conducted with successful business leaders, we are told that what took most time was to find the objective that everyone found appealing and which could only be realised by everyone cooperating. They have dedicated their time in talking and listening to employees, managers, partner companies, and other stakeholders, in order to establish the objective. This is the most important investment for any company wanting to dismantle their silos; that of seeking, finding, and using the magnet that can pull the entire organisation forward.

Passion, meaning and collectivity

When something is meaningful, our energy is limitless, creating a pull-effect, but when there is no meaning behind something there is no passion or driving force and the push-effect has to be used. A higher meaning in what we do, combined with passion, could be the quick formula for how to navigate the new platforms. We cannot talk about passionate employees if there is nothing to get them empassioned. Top management has a responsibility for creating a conducive framework for this by using superordinate goals. Napolean Bonaparte was highly skilled in human psychology and creating social bonds. He knew that no one is willing to give their life for a bag of money, but will gladly fight long and hard for *"a band of coloured ribbon"* as he put it, cynically. The ribbon which Bonaparte refers to is the mark of honour which a soldier would receive for service to their country.

In companies driven by the structure and mechanics of silos, it is not people's needs that are given top priority, but rather, the companies' desire to maximise profit. But profit doesn't fulfill human desire for recognition, and nowhere in the accounts can we see evidence that the companies' activities are meaningful for those employed. When driven only by the logics of profit, the focus will be on the machine's production and output instead of whether the cogs and levers are good and healthy. The employees' performance and ability to increase production is seen as more important than why they are working in the first place. A keynote speaker once asked a group of business people: "How many of you have making money as your mission?" A mass of hands were raised in the air. "So, if I now put the money in your hands that you aim to earn this year, what is your mission?" A stark silence hit the room. No one knew what to answer.

Simon Sinek, the author of *Start With Why*, does not believe that a company's mission is to trade with people who need the product they produce. This explains only what the company does, and not why they do it. Sinek believes that the mission first becomes attractive when one can explain the reason and meaning for what the company does. In this way, the mission becomes trading with people who believe in what you believe in. Therefore, as a business leader, you must be able to explain *why* you do what you do so that the customer can decide whether this is meaningful for *them* or not. Maybe the customer will be just as passionate when us-

"An 'organization' is but an idea – a concept. People, as individuals, are the ultimate reality and the only operative element. An idea cannot make a commitment to anything or take responsibility or action – only individuals can."

– Chris Rufer, The Morning Star Company

ing the product, as the company's leadership and employees are when they present it. Apple's products, for example, ooze this passion. The love affair Mac users have with their phone or computer is based on intuition. Apple's products are developed on the basis of *why* and not only *what*. There is a difference, and it makes a difference if you manage to create passion and meaning and, as such, contríbute to a higher purpose.

The same applies to salary when considered as a force of attraction or motivation. Salary has an operative function in supporting the exchange of services. But an increase in salary in fact becomes demotivating. Yes! You read this correctly.

In his book *Drive*, Daniel Pink described an experiment done at MIT which investigated what motivates people. The experiment was carried out by Professor Karim Lakhani and management consultant, Bob Wolf. They began with the assumption that we people are most motivated by money and that the more money we make, the more motivated we become. But the research indicated that this wasn't always the case. There are two key exceptions in which money is still a motivating factor. The first is if we are at the bottom of Maslow's pyramid and cannot survive if we don't make money. The second is if we are doing routine work, that is, performing a mechanical task which relies on our hands rather than our brains. Employees who receive a salary that satisfies their basic needs are not motivated by money for completing a task which requires their most simple cognitive functions. On the contrary, in these cases, money can appear negative and demotivating. Since this result at MIT was so radically different from expected, it was decided to repeat it in India. But again, the results were the same. The more money people were given to motivate them in tasks that demanded them to think for themselves, the more *demotivated* the person became! The experiment showed that two factors were instrumental in creating motivation: first, the freedom to make decisions, steering one's own path instead of merely being subject to lots of external rules; second, the opportunity for development and personal growth, a desire to be better at what one does and become the best version of oneself. In spite of not being paid for it, there is apparently a strong desire to develop. Researchers Karim Lakhani and Bob Wolf concluded that: "Positive motivation, determined by how creative someone *feels* when they are working on a project, is the strongest and most long-lasting *driver*." The World Value Surveys' annual scoping of wellbeing and value in different countries, aligns to Lakhani and Wolf's findings in concluding that an individual's level of happiness is determined by the amount of freedom they have for making their own decisions. In other words when a company's leadership wants to operate from a platform, they should begin by setting up some clear overriding objectives, which they themselves and their employees are passionate about. With this done, the leadership should then give their middle management and employees the freedom to find their own means of meeting the objectives.

In Scandinavia, we are well-experienced in creating platforms that are rich in trust. The Danes are not only the happiest nation in the world, but also the most trusting. Therefore, it is obvious for us to base our business and leadership models on trust, freedom, and enabling people to make their own decisions. Most of us go to work to fulfill our need for recognition, respect, and self-actualisation. We want to demonstrate our passion and our highest potential, and according to Maslow, we are only happy when this is possible. People who seek self-actualisation feel deeply connected to their social and environmental context. Silos offer neither freedom, meaning nor opportunity for development. The rigid mechanics of industrialism has put a stop to these kind of motivating factors. As a result, it is not so strange that the business culture of the silos is now characterised by stress, inertia, and lack of meaning.

Small and intimate is beautiful

"Small is beautiful" is, as mentioned in Chapter One, the mantra that economist and adviser for the National Coal Board, E.F Schumacher argued for in the 1970s. Schumacher was an inspiration to many international leaders, including Jimmy Carter, who called on his advice once he was made President of the United States. In Schumacher's book, "Small is beautiful" (1973), he develops his theory that large entities cease to be effective over a certain size. For example, he explains that when a company gets too big, its employees start to lose track of its meaning as they lose their overview and connection to the whole. Let us go a little deeper into this mindset, because when we begin to organise ourselves on platforms, we should ask how big these should be?

On the basis of his research, the British anthropologist, Robin Dunbar, proposes that there is a direct relationship between the size of the outer layer of the cerebrum, in the human brain, and how big a group can be for the individual to feel and perform at their best. The size of our brain determines how many people with whom we can have stable interpersonal relationships. Dunbar concluded that the average human brain size could cope with a maximum of 148 people. Dunbar's social analysis was also conducted by the company, Goretex, and they reached a similar result, that 150 people was the optimum size for a large but still well-functioning group. Following this analysis, Bill Gore, the founder of Gore-Tex, decided to make this the limit for the number of personnel in his factories. When the company needed to expand, he built a new factory. These smaller factories generated a better feeling of belonging and showed a higher morale amongst employees. Dunbar claims that, in the context of our modern, advanced, and highly technological society, we need to increase our feeling of community and social belonging. We need to be part of something bigger than ourselves. The optimal environment for people is a small community, where close relationships can blossom and where we can trust each other. Small communities can work together with others toward the same overriding objective. The conclusion is that our platform can only accommodate a limited number of individuals. When we go beyond this number, we must then create a new platform which is still linked to the original one, but which becomes self-sufficient.

Our brains determine how well we function in the company of others. In his book *The Empathic Civilization*, Jeremy Rifkin writes that the way in which our brain is structured, affecting how we feel, think, and act, is out of sync with the world we have created for ourselves. We need a change in our external world so that it corresponds to the way our internal world works. We are equipped with mirror neurons which allow us to feel the pain, delight, or discomfort which others around us experience, but without us taking on the pain as our own. This ability to empathize allows us to navigate as a group. If we don't act in a way that works for the group then, via our mirror neurons, we become emotional ly affected by the parts of the organisation that don't work. Mirror neurons are part of the feedback system which allows us to sense automatically highs and lows in the well-being of our environment. This means that when, for example, we try not to let a neighbour's conflict bother us, it will have its affect on us anyway. This is why it is important that, when on the new platforms, we can embrace how other people are feeling. According to Rifkin, our empathy can be the most important *"invisible hand"* in making sure that our society can function.

It isn't only Rifkin who describes the need in people to make sure that others are happy. The same beliefs are voiced by the author to *"The Invisible Hand"*, Adam Smith, in his *"Theory of Moral Sentiments"* from 1759. He writes: "When someone has a passion for something, then the thought of he who has the passion will be felt physically in the chest of all attentive listeners." Smith believed that it is our ability to feel empathy for others that forms the basis of our moral conduct. In his lifetime though, the world was by no means as well-connected as it is today, meaning that empathy was limited to a population or grouping of modest size. Perhaps it is therefore that Smith concluded: "We will therefore only be slightly interested in those people who we can neither serve or harm and which nature has cleverly located in a place far from our own."

If a Nordic company produces its goods in India, for example, it is this physical distance that, according to Adam Smith, can result in lower levels of empathy and therefore, also, moral conduct. The further away someone suffers harm as a result of defects in the production process, then the less empathy will be felt by the company's employees, and the easier it will be for them to denounce responsibility for the situation. The Internet and other global network forms have decreased the distance between far away and close by. An example is the accident of April 2013, in which over 1100 textile workers in Dhaka, Bangladesh were killed when their building collapsed. When pictures of the dead and wounded, being carried out of the ruins, were shown on screens in the Nordic latitudes, empathy and responsibility grew to the fore. Many companies who had sourced clothes from the factories in this building paid compensation despite the fact that many were not legally obliged to do so. Empathy for the suppliers and stakeholders in Bangladesh won over regulation. The lesson to learn here is that neither a platform's scope nor social network are limited by legal obligation.

In order to function well in a social context and as the leaders and employees of a company, we are drawn to behave in a way that doesn't harm the people or environment around us. If a business leader doesn't recognise such human needs, this can yield fatal consequences in terms of the survival of the company. Compassion and empathy are essential in finding the solutions that can contribute to the whole and, in so doing so, allow the entire company to run effectively. The level of empathy becomes an important means of measuring a company's ability to take responsibility for theirs suppliers, for example. If this had happened in Bangladesh, the accident could well have been avoided. The Internet has created transparency with regard to corporate behaviour. To maintain their good reputation, businesses need to keep a closer eye on their operations. A negative story can quickly come out to a critical mass of customers. This happened in 2005, to *United Brands* who own the lingerie chain, *Victoria's Secret*. The American NGO, *Forest Ethics,* put *Victoria's Secret* under the spotlight when they discovered them to be printing their catalogues from paper sourced from endangered forests in Canada. *Victoria's Secret* released around 350 million catalogues per year without applying environmental standards to their production. The company was finally exposed in a full page advertisement in the *New York Times* with the headline, "Victoria's Dirty Secret". This escalated into an enormous press coverage that, in turn, lead to demonstrations outside the stores and a boycott of the products. *United Brands* has, since this time, worked together with *Forest Ethics* in defining a rigorous set of environmental standards which now apply to the production of their catalogues.

Our inborn human need to behave rightly and justly, coupled with our common sense and empathy can support sustainable development if companies can manage to lead and organise themselves to match current needs and challenges. When a company has a higher purpose than only making money, and when it conducts itself justly and with empathy, then people feel that this is a good place to work or do business. This happens when the mirror neurons of employees, customers, suppliers and other stakeholders are positively activated. When a business has this higher purpose as its mission and driver, then it can readily serve our whole society *and* make money.

Elements for the new platform – *Summary*
- The platform makes it possible to create something bigger than the individual silos by allowing synergies to occur.
- Leaders and employees on a platform need a *"superordinate goal"* which everyone wants to support and which can only be achieved when all individuals work together.
- Meaning is created by having a *why*. This is the platform's primary vehicle towards healthy and sustainable growth.
- The way to profit is passion and meaning in what one does. These are the primary drivers in reaching all goals.
- The goal is everything living and dynamic which creates profit; namely, the happiness and well-being of the employees.
- You get motivation and happiness on the platform by allowing freedom and enabling self-organising development to occur. Motivation is not reached by giving out more money.
- Your platform should hold a maximum of 150 people.
- The platform won't work effectively unless everyone is content.

THE OPEN SEAS

"If you want to build a ship, then you shouldn't just assemble people to collect wood, divide the work and give out orders. You should instead give them the desire for the open seas."

– Antoine de Saint-Exupéry

CHAPTER 5

The philosophy behind the platforms

In this chapter, we will look at the philosophy or mindset that drives the new platforms. You will be given an insight into the beliefs and preconceptions which should be put to rest and which ones to develop in order to serve us better in the future. You will be shown that the competitive advantage we have in Scandinavia is not that we are faster, better, or cheaper than others, but that we are good at working together and taking responsibility for the bigger picture. The cornerstone of our platform philosophy is the conviction that what we can achieve together is greater and more important than what we can achieve individually, and that we dare to cooperate and share because we trust one another.

Our beliefs shape our reality

The American anthropologist Gregory Bateson discovered that if we don't manage to change the beliefs that define us as people, then the effects of competence and behaviour remain unchanged too. It is our beliefs that drive us and which also determine how our culture is shaped. When we step out onto the platform with the same beliefs we had in the silo, we will end in the same place we just left; that is, back in the silo again. Albert Einstein was searching for a new mindset to shape new systems. Many are aware of his famous words, *"We cannot solve our problems with the same thinking that created them."* Let us therefore take some time to look at the five levels in Bateson's culture pyramid, which outlines the values, philosophies, and beliefs which can create a new mindset and a new consciousness (see fig.5 on page 97).

All organisations and systems have a culture and Gregory Bateson's model explains the constituent elements. At the top of the pyramid is identity an individual's or an organisation's. Next layer down is our values. These determine the knowledge and competences we seek. In turn, these determine our behaviour. Finally, our behaviour determines the basic characteristics of the environment we create in our organisations or companies. This environment is the bottom layer of the pyramid.

In other words, our values and beliefs are the basic driving forces for our actions. If a business leader is of the belief that it is necessary to control his employees' performance, then he will introduce tools so that he can check up on them. When employees are met with distrust and put under surveillance, they simply mirror the distrust and hostility that is shown towards them. They don't want anyone to find fault in them. They want to show that they are working in the right way and as they should. They want to keep themselves to themselves. Their working environment will be affected by this in that employees will appear protective and defensive. Each will only want to bake a cake for themselves. The organisation will become marked by a lack of knowledge and cooperation. People will keep to their own discipline and will be punished for stepping beyond its limits. If the business leader organises an open office layout, in the hope that this will encourage his employees to work more together, then they will still uphold the same skill-set as before and the same introvert behaviour. In other words, their conviction to stay within their silo will simply move with them.

It won't help to drag people out of their silos, place them in an open office and assume that this, in itself, will increase cooperation and the feeling of community. In this case, it is only the surroundings that change. Nothing has changed at the higher levels of the culture pyramid. If, as their leader, I believe that my employees' motivation will increase and their skill-set will sharpen when I show them trust and grant them the freedom to do as they see best, then they will perform with trust. A company directed in this way, will seek those competences that best prepare the employees to de-

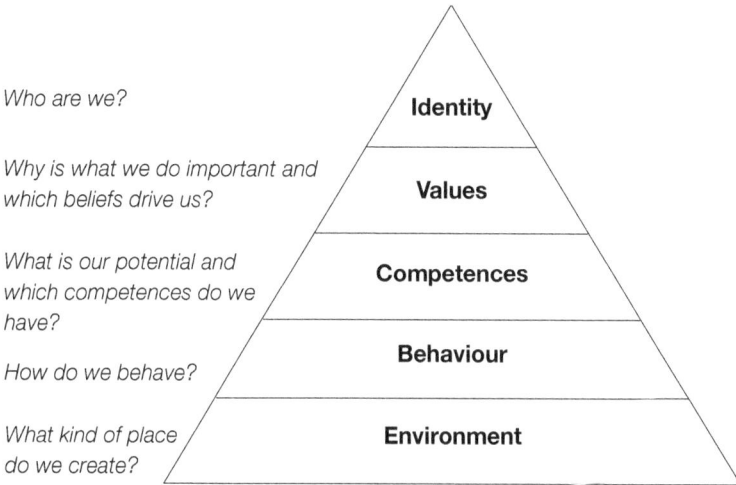

Who are we? — **Identity**

Why is what we do important and which beliefs drive us? — **Values**

What is our potential and which competences do we have? — **Competences**

How do we behave? — **Behaviour**

What kind of place do we create? — **Environment**

Based on anthropologist, Gregory Bateson's cultural pyramid.

velop and solve any given task. The preferred behaviour is one in which input, feedback, and empowerment from others can support each employee to do their jobs to the best of their ability. The work environment, as a whole, will be characterised by meaningful relationships and a community atmosphere. The three motivating factors outlined earlier - self-sufficiency, development, and meaning - will become part of the culture.

Getting new beliefs under our skin

Cultural change within business is a great challenge. We cannot learn to take on different values or beliefs in the same way as we can learn new skills or new ways to behave. Beliefs are like DNA, an inborn part of us that is created by our environment, upbringing, education, and experiences. These conditions cannot just be erased and replaced with new ones. We all know business leaders who have been on training courses to learn new skills or behaviours, for example, *Leading With Recognition*. When they return to their organisation and try to apply the lessons learned in practice, this often doesn't feel authentic. Maybe the business leader thinks in exactly the same way as before; for example, that people get money for their work and that recognition doesn't belong to the world of business. We cannot exactly pin down what makes the situation seem contrived, when one's director or manager suddenly begins to recognise their surroundings, but it feels false to accept this new recognition.

The expression, *"lip service"* is used to describe what happens when someone does something they don't truly believe in, but which they have heard could be to their benefit. Their lips say one thing, but they believe something else. When people don't have the values and beliefs to justify certain forms of behaviour or types of compentence, then they lack authenticity or alignment between brain, heart, and hands.

I have arrived at this insight through the experience of teaching several hundred tasks and staying aware throughout their processes. Today, before starting to teach new skills, I always look at what lies in the background in terms of values and beliefs. If I don't do this, then I cannot engage the person in transformation or cultural change, which means that no change is genuine or lasting.

If we go back to the person mentioned earlier, who believed that we would all fight over a bag of money, the competences his beliefs support are about being fastest, best, and cheapest. Such competences will be reflected in his behaviour. He will tend to keep his cards close to his chest. His behaviour will create an environment made up of silos and containing individuals who compete against each other. My experience is that there are three ways to change such a person's beliefs:

– Via the head. We can show documented research that his way of thinking no longer works. We can, for example, illustrate real cases in which others have succeeded in new

ventures by changing their beliefs and way of thinking. This is an appeal to his rational intelligence or IQ.
- Via the heart. Using history, film and other media, we can let him sense how both old and new beliefs *feel*. This is an appeal to his emotional intelligence or "EQ".
- Via the hand. We can let him use his physical intelligence or "PQ" in completing practical exercises (such as, making the cake bigger; *see fig. 3, page 79*).

People learn differently, but by using head, heart, and hand all at once, we can increase the magnitude and permanence of the effect.

The person who assumed that we would all fight over the bag of money, ended by working whole-heartedly with partner cooperations in the building sector. He discovered, via negotiation exercises and mediation training, the benefits of working together. Another individual I'd met and who became very angry when his beliefs were challenged, contacted me one year after our acquaintance to say that now he had made the changes we talked about. At first, I didn't realise that it was the same man who had been sitting on the front row at my talk and had been so provoked by what I'd said. It isn't an easy process to change beliefs and culture. The stronger the beliefs, the stronger the opposition. It takes time before the new beliefs can sit comfortably in our head, heart, and body.

New platforms first come about when we begin to work with our values and beliefs, and when we decide that we want to shape a new culture. Most of us in the Western world find ourselves at the top of Maslow's pyramid where we seek to fulfil our needs for self-actualisation and altruism. We dream of living in an environment which doesn't differentiate between our external and internal worlds, where identity and a sense of belonging are top priorities, and where work has become an integrated and natural part of us because it has meaning. Employees are no longer thought of as hired hands, but as whole beings with souls and feelings. According to Maslow, employees want to be met with an appreciation that they are reliable, that they seek responsibility and meaning in their work, and that they want to learn and develop. Furthermore, that they are not adverse to change, are resilient to manipulation, and prefer to work over being unemployed.

When old beliefs die and new ones are born

Working with culture can appear to be daunting. One shouldn't underestimate just how much time and energy is required to build an organisation's culture. However, when the beliefs are in place, they will work for the organisation like a magnet attracting everyone and driving employees in the same direction.

VISA spent two years articulating their beliefs, intentions, and meaning. Former founder and CEO, Dee Hock, tells us: "We are living at a time when a 400-year old identity is dying and another one is struggling to be born - a change of culture, knowledge, society, and institutions greater than the world has ever seen. In front of us lies a unique opportunity to regenerate our individuality, freedom, collectivity and ethics. There is a big potential to reach a harmony between nature, each other and a spiritual intelligence which the world could never have dreamt of."

In other words, there are old systems which are beginning to change. All the same, it shouldn't surprise us that our dependency to, and our belief in, these systems is deeply. There is a critical paradox between, on the one hand, our need for freedom, and on the other hand, our need for order. An organisation will often move back and forth between these two extremes: One pole, steered by extreme control, comes to life in the silos and via command and control systems. The other pole, steered by extreme freedom, comes to its own as chaos, a lack of common direction and a state of anarchy. In times of crisis, and motivated by fear, companies and their chief executives have used economics to tighten their belts via command and control systems. Many people experience that during crisis they are pushed downwards in

Maslow's pyramid of needs. Many desire the comfort that comes when others tell them what to do. But a tight-fit management is not the way forward. The new platform contains elements of both order and chaos or, to use other words, cooperation and competition. The platform itself helps us to deal with this duality since it offers both more space to move and more tolerance.

Dee Hock, who was the brains behind VISA's concept for making cardholders into owners of the business, calls their particular system, *chaordic*. The system contains a mix of order and chaos. This is the kind of mix we see within nature. There are elements which cause *flow* (growth), *flex* (connectivity) and *form* (sustainability). Dee Hock makes his own definition for the word, *chaord*: "By *chaord*, I mean all self-organising, adaptive, non-linear, complex systems, regardless of whether they are physical, biological or social, and which are characterised by both order and chaos, or in business terminology; cooperation and competition."

The company which Dee Hock created in 1970 has grown in the order of ten thousand percent and continues to expand by around twenty percent per year. Today, VISA operates in 200 countries across the world and serves half a billion customers.

Dee Hock talks about developing a design which follows the principles of self-organising systems, between cooperation and competition, between order and chaos, and between flow and form. The aim is to find the area of synergy where such opposites can meet and then function as a whole. The different poles are kept together by allowing a generous flexibility to occur between the two. The premise is that it is easier to work with opposing methods as long as there is a force which can connect them. We can see this kind of opposition in all natural systems. If we succeed in creating a system based on *flow* (growth), *flex* (connectivity) and *form* (sustainability), we can then create a prosperous organisation which can keep on serving both others and itself, long-term.

Over the past ten years, Dee Hock and MIT Professor, Peter Senge, have been working on creating a business model to accommodate the opposition between order and chaos. The mindset behind the chaordic model is the same as for a decentralised model. Dee Hock describes the key principles in his article, *"The Chaordic Organization: Out of Control and Into Order"* (1995):

- The organisation needs to be equally owned by all parties. No one person should be given more importance or priority over the others. Every benefit should be the direct consequence of an individual's skill and initiative.
- Power and projects should be equally distributed. No task should be done by a centralised part of the whole, if it can be done by a decentralised part. No authority should fall to a centralised part of the whole, if it can be assumed by a decentralised part.
- The leadership should be distributed. No one individual, no institution or any single combination of these should be allowed to dominate the beliefs or steer decisions.
- The organisation must always be flexible and robust. It must be able to be keep itself afloat, allow for changes to occur but not allow itself to lose track of its own nature or core principles.
- The organisation must accommodate diversity and change. It must attract people and institutions who are happy with these conditions and who can create a culture of well-being and mutual support.

The qualities listed above are based on the conviction that the best decisions are those which are taken as close to the source as possible and that responsibility should be positioned as far towards the bottom levels of the organisation as possible. No director or manager should make a decision which can be taken further down in the organisation. Every time you, as a leader, make a decision for someone who could actually have taken it themselves, you push the person and the organisation one step backwards. Granting responsibility to the employees gives them the chance of satisfaction and contentment because they can make their own decisions, they are able to develop, and they are free to put content to the framework in the way they consider best.

On our new platform, we need to decentralise as far to the boundaries as possible and we need to work with the key element of flow, flex, and form. The qualities inherent in these three elements has already been described; namely that nothing is static and everyone is constantly in flux. It is essential to maintain the flexibility between flow and form; in other words, between context and content. Change is a condition of life and organisations must be able to work within a changing world. A *chaordic* system is unfortunately not a model which companies can suddenly implement, but the values and convictions at its foundations are vital to know if you want to move your organisation from a silo-based mindset to a platform-based mindset.

Flow is growth without the fight

When we talk about growth today, as a rule we are referring to economic growth. Economic growth is important for a society's development, but so too are other forms of growth because growth gives dynamism and flow. Many assume that growth can only be created with blood, sweat and tears. On a platform, however, flow is the same as say, a growth in health and, as such, becomes a natural development for which we don't need to sacrifice our well-being by driving ourselves into the ground. Flow is the natural drive which everyone has within them, as a consequence of a desire to keep growing and developing. If we didn't have this drive, we wouldn't survive. The same applies to businesses, organisations, and systems. They must change and develop with time if they are to function well and serve human needs. An organisation separated by silos is a static and rigid system.

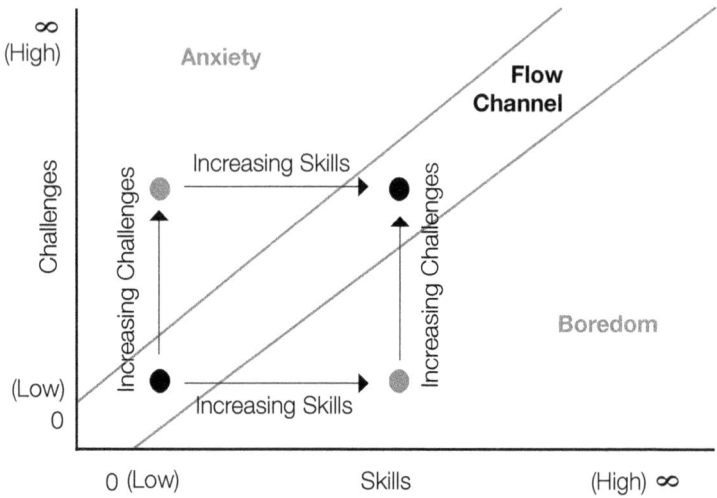

Source: Anxiety, Boredom and Flow, Csikszentmihalyi (1990)

It is time to bid it farewell as it no longer serves our needs. An organisation built on platforms can serve our needs as a result of its flexibility, assuming that there is widespread consensus with regard to the purpose behind what we are working for and towards.

Leadership and employees must, on the one hand, hold onto their purpose whilst, on the other hand, stay flexible with regard to how to achieve it. We often think that we can plan a route from A to B, but in reality, the route is much less direct. Leaders and employees must be able to accept certain *detours* since they can, in fact, turn out to be better routes to reaching one's goal. This is what flow is about.

The term flow was defined by a Hungarian professor in psychology, Mihaly Csikszentmihalyi, to describe the mental condition we find ourselves in when our energy level is high and we are completely absorbed in something. When we feel success within a working process, we often lose track of time and place. Sometimes, we may also get a feeling of euphoria. When we experience this kind of flow, then the work we do doesn't feel like hard or demanding labour.

According to Mihaly Csikszentmihalyi, there are three preconditions for this kind of flow. First, the work one is engaged in needs to have a clear purpose which gives structure and direction to the task. Second, there must be a good balance between the challenges one expects to find and the competences one feels one can apply. One needs to trust that they are able to complete the task. Third, the task needs to give immediate and clear feedback. This can help us to negotiate changing demands and allow us to adjust our efforts in order to maintain the flow.

In order for flow to exist in a company, its infrastructure needs to contain the same qualities as the chaordic system. This means; a maximum overview and a high degree of responsibility for each employee, no more than 150 people, and immediate feedback.

If we are subjected to too much pressure, for example, if the challenge gets too great, we become anxious and can no longer work effectively. If we are given too little responsibility we start to get bored.

Figure 6 shows flow as a motion between anxiety and boredom, dependent on one's skills and the challenges one faces. If we want a company to perform to its optimum, but still without stress, then we need to construct a platform in order to channel the right flow. That growth can only come from competition is an assumption we need to eradicate. A company that chooses, on the other hand, to operate on a platform, must be driven by a superordinate goal, allowing growth to occur as a natural flow and without putting its employees under unreasonable amounts of pressure.

CSR

Mads Øvlisen, former CEO for Novo and member of the UN's Global Compact Board has said: "You shouldn't work

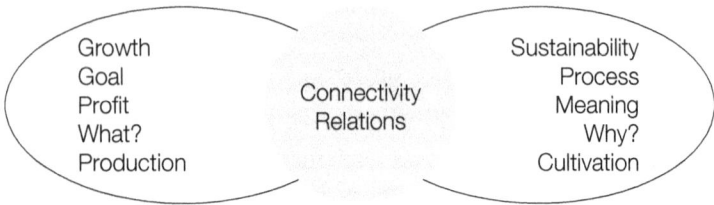

Growth		Sustainability
Goal		Process
Profit	Connectivity	Meaning
What?	Relations	Why?
Production		Cultivation

with CSR to earn money. You should work with CSR because you believe in it, and *then* you can begin to earn money."

This belief is shared by the founder of Whole Foods Market, John Mackey. He says, "Long-term profit is maximised by making this the primary goal." A third way to express the same belief comes from Abraham Maslow: "You won't get happy by seeking happiness. You get happy by seeking to do something meaningful."

If you look at figure 7, the platform begins on the right "wing" and not on the left, as a traditional silo-based organisation would.

CSR shouldn't be an add-on to a company. It shouldn't either be placed in its own department. Instead, CSR must be the company's heart, value base, belief, and *superordinate goal*. Responsibility and sustainability are not only about being good and doing good. The company's purpose must be that it serves the whole. If it doesn't do this, then it won't manage to keep generating profit. A business is intrinsically linked to its environment. As Joseph Bragdon describes in his book *Profit for Life*: "Economy is part of a larger ecological system and we can't keep on avoiding this." This is common sense.

There is no need to talk about CSR on a platform since it is simply part of the company's heart and purpose. In an analysis conducted by the Economist Intelligence Unit, *"Management Magnified, Sustainability and Corporate Growth"* (2009), different companies reported that sustainability could well give them a competitive advantage, but that if sustainability and CSR initiatives were badly implemented, this could have a negative effect on the business. When CSR and sustainable growth are a company's framework and superordinate goal, implementation will happen naturally as an integrated part of the company's overall strategy. Here, we get back to Mads Øvlisen: one needs genuinely to believe in CSR in order to attain economic benefit. The conviction that one has a shared responsibility for the whole (system or society) is critical on a platform and CSR can never be defined, created, or communicated from just one department, or silo. CSR *is* the business.

Creating shared value

Creating shared value (CSV) is a term which supports the idea that CSR is a fully integrated part of a company's mindset. CSV was first articulated in the Harvard Business Review, in December 2006, in the article *"Strategy and Society: The Link between Competitive Advantage and Corporate Social Responsibility"*. From here, the article *"Creating Shared Value: Redefining Capitalism and the Role of the Corporation in Society"*, expanded on the term's usage and relevance. The men behind the term and mindset are Michael E. Porter, Head of the Institute for Strategy and Competitiveness at Harvard Business School, and Mark R. Kramer, Senior Fellow of the Kennedy School at Harvard University. Porter and Kramer are spokesmen for what they consider to be the next big transformation in leadership thinking; namely that businesses incorporate social relations in their purpose, strategy and operations. As such, they want to redefine CSR (corporate social responsibility) as CSV (creating shared value).

Shared values are commercial strategies or practices that can improve a company's competitiveness, whilst, at the same time, improving the social and economic conditions in the society in which they operate. The benefit gained by society is that it will be able to develop faster. The bene-

"I don't know what your destiny will be, but one thing I do know: the only ones among you who will be really happy are those who have sought and found how to serve".

– Albert Schweitzer

fit gained by the company is faster growth. When the surrounding society is more developed, the company has a better chance of experiencing growth. This shapes a good circle in which benefit is mutual. The company and society meet in synergy. Together, they make up the whole. John Mackey works with similar principles in his concept for *Conscious Capitalism*, where he suggests that a success in society should be used as a measure of success in a company. This conviction is a fundamental basis for the new platform. The conviction should ensure holism and connectivity between the company and society.

Handelsbanken can be proud of the fact that their way of doing business has lifted the motivation and well-being of their employees instead of holding them back. People should never make decisions for others who are capable of deciding for themselves. When the CEO at the time, Jan Wallander (read his interview, page 45) decided in the summer of 1970 that all decisions being taken at head office should be transferred back to the many small branches, this caused a huge outcry from the support and controller functions in middle management. Support functions could no longer send instructions down in the hierarchy and afterwards control whether they had been carried out properly. Instead, they should provide feedback on the tasks in hand and make different resources available as and when required by the branch offices. The support functions were convinced that such radical changes would never work and that they could result in drastic consequences. 60 people in head office were asked to leave in exchange for a job out in a smaller branch office.

The process took five years. After this time, all responsibility which could be delegated locally was delegated. There were only a few tasks which could not logically be decentralised. As such, currency exchange, contract work, and international banking were retained within head office.

What was the motivation and basis for such a big decision? Partly, this had to do with profits having hit a record low. Partly, it was to do with Wallander's belief that a business should be led in support of human nature and not against it. This was also the title of his book, *"Med den manskliga natur – inte mot" ("With human nature, not against it")*. Human nature strives for responsibility, development and meaning, or as Wallander puts it "trust and respect", which make up the second highest layer in Maslow's pyramid of needs.

Positioning responsibility in head office creates a distance between brain and hand, in other words between those who conceive ideas and make decisions and those who implement the work. When we decentralise we can reconnect brain and hand. The people who create the strategy or project, also implement it. This gives meaning and contentment as well as trust and respect. It can also lead to significant savings for the company since existing resources and competences can be used more effectively and the doubling-up of manpower can be avoided.

As described earlier, it takes time to find the right purpose. It took VISA a year for them to find their focus and it took time before the story of Handelsbanken, *"Goals, means and philosophy"* ("Mål, midler og filosofi") came to light. The book describes how Handelsbanken achieved greater profitability and effectiveness than their competitors by allowing their employees to make most decisions themselves. As Wallander kept acknowledging during the interview, the philosophy builds upon good, common sense.

The employees are rewarded for the results they achieve for the bank, not in the form of an end of year bonus, but via a pension contribution called *Oktogon*. In this way, the bank avoids cash bonuses becoming an ineffective incentive for motivation. Today, Handelsbanken is one of the largest banks in Scandinavia. Since their transformation they have managed to live up to their economic goal of a higher than average profitability when compared to other banks in their market. The bank is very close to becoming Denmark's fourth largest and is already the most expenditure efficient bank in Europe. When we look at customer satisfaction polls in Scandinavia, Handelsbanken comes out at the very top of the list.

When implementing a model such as the one adopted by Handelsbanken, it is vital that all elements of the model are put in place. One cannot just take the parts one is most fond of and assume things will work. Having chosen to decentralise, removing budgets and controls comes automatically because these don't make sense in a decentralised model. The secret and driving force behind Handelsbanken's success is decentralisation. It is all one package, one system, and must be considered holistically. If one begins to doubt something in the system, one must return to the purpose. From here, one must make the necessary changes to ensure that the intention behind the system can be maintained long-term, regardless of future adjustments and the inbuilt flexibility which will allow for them.

So, why hasn't the *blue ocean strategy*, which has granted Handelsbanken forty years of success, been copied by other Nordic banks or companies? The Scandinavians are amongst the most trusting people in the world, so why haven't others decentralised, handing power back to the individual employee just as Handelsbanken has done? Is this because it is so difficult to surrender one's power once it has been won? After all, "Turkeys don't vote for Thanksgiving!" Despite Scandinavia having the lowest gap between rich and poor, we still live in a hierarchy where power and status are important. The same hierarchy is seen in organisations whose diagrams show clearly who is at the top and who is at the bottom. As long as we maintain a hierarchical structure in our organisations, there will always be the fight to reach the top and then, having got there, a desire to hold onto power and authority. A vital factor in Wallander's success in building a decentralised organisation was the support he got from the board of directors. The board didn't listen to the directors who complained about losing their power.

Becoming worthy of leadership

In a silo or hierarchy, the movement goes from top to bottom. The bottom is locked into completing tasks in accordance with instructions they are given from above. If they do as they are told, they are rewarded. If not, they are punished. Bonus and motivation is given in the form of money or promotion higher up in the system. Top and bottom are bound together by control channels which ensure that instructions issued from the top are carried out properly. If not, then word is sent back up to the top, from where new orders are issued down again on how to get things back on track. The more detailed the instructions are, the more senseless and difficult it becomes to understand and implement them. This prompts the need for even more instructions to keep people on track towards the goal.

In such a system, managers and directors are picked by top leadership. The managers promoted are those who have proved best at carrying out and implementing orders. In contrast, on a platform, neither managers, directors, nor anyone else is given a "stick" to keep people in line. Similarly, there is no "carrot" to tempt people along because we know that handing out bonuses is not an effective method to raise motivation. People work at their best when they have the freedom to follow a meaningful goal which they have understood and adopted as their own. On the platform, all leaders must create a drive and passion to work from the inside out by setting the superordinate goal which everyone can believe in.

One needs to become worthy of leadership. Loyalty and trust must come from the employees themselves. As such, the first employee to put their faith in you and want to fol-

Who am I? — **Identity**

Why is what I do important and which beliefs drive me? — **Values**

What is my potential and which competences do I have? — **Competences**

How do I behave? — **Behaviour**

What context do I create? — **Environment**

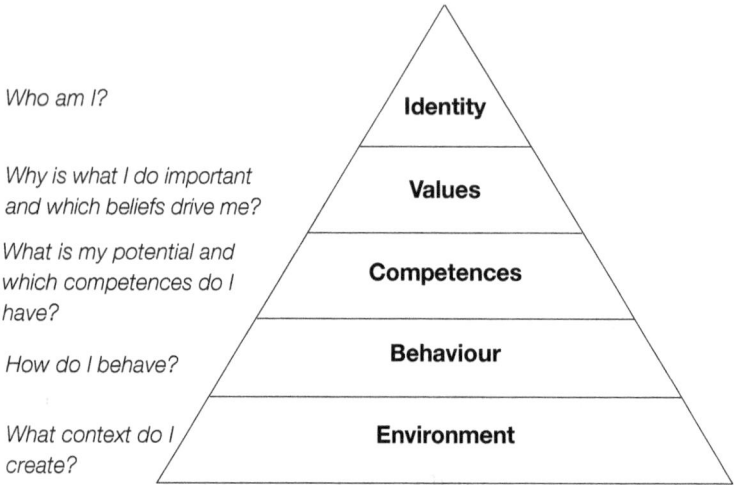

Anthropologist Gregory Bateson's Cultural Pyramid shown here with respect to leadership qualities

low your lead is, in fact, more important than you yourself. It is your job as leader to serve your employees so that they can work at their best, and, as Wallander highlights, it is the job of head office to serve the smaller branches. Social entrepreneur, Derek Sivers, who works to meet society's social and environmental needs, said the following in his TED talk: "The first business companion is the one who transforms you from lonely fool to leader."

Brazilian Ricardo Semler took over the family business, SEMCO, from his father in 1982. At just 21 years old, Semler had some radical ideas that he wanted to bring in, but which his father was dead against. All the same, Ricardo succeeded in persuading his father to give him steer over the company. Ricardo wanted to introduce a leadership where the employees themselves chose their leader and set the level of each other's salary. Now, perhaps you are thinking that this is far too alternative, and simply wouldn't be possible for a business. When Ricardo took over SEMCO, they had 90 employees and an annual turnover of 4 million dollars. By 2003, they had 3000 employees and annual turnover had risen to 212 million dollars. This expansion was a result of Semler's so-called industrial democracy. The model builds on the conviction that people will only follow someone whom they respect, and that it is the culture and individual employee who can determine the best person to lead. To aid this kind of selection in occurring from the bottom upwards, the employees interview their potential leader before his employment and afterwards evaluate him every six months. It is not unheard of today to evaluate one's boss, but this kind of selection process is very rare. Ricardo Semler continued to go against the current by involving his employees in discussing what a reasonable salary would be for fellow employees. The story is told in the book, "*Maverick!: The Success Story Behind the World's Most Unusual Workplace*" written by Ricardo Semler and has sold over one million copies.

Leader qualities on the platform

Before you read on, I'd like to ask you two questions and set you a task for you to assess where you stand as a leader.

1. Would you get the same [behavior? treatment? respect?] from your colleagues if you didn't have your job title?
2. Would you get the same [behavior? treatment? respect?] from your colleagues if you weren't able to use sanctions or penalties?

If you answer "yes" to these two questions, you have the potential to be a leader on the platform. Try now to answer this question: "What would Bateson's pyramid look like (fig. 8) if you were to fill in each layer to describe your form of leadership on the platform?"

Leadership on a platform resembles geese, which always fly in a V-formation. The bird at the front leads the way. The other geese trust and respect the goose in front. They en-

"When I made the concept in 1976, those in Älm-hult were convinced that nothing in the world could change it. Only if we were one hundred percent sure that we had made a mistake, could we consider changing it. Otherwise, there was nothing to discuss. When people argue for other solutions, we listen and try to fit the argument to the framework. The framework is sacred and fixed but inside it, there is plenty of freedom and space for ideas to bounce around. No retail store should be the same as another."

- Ingvar Kamprad, IKEA's founder and owner.
Extract from the book, "Kamprads lilla gulblå"

courage him with their cries as their leader begins to tire. When the leader is too tired to continue, another goose takes its place, allowing the first to fall back in the formation and regain the energy they put in to pulling the flock forward. Keeping in the V-formation gives the geese 70 percent more flying power. The group offers greater value, which can only be utilized by working together and keeping leadership inclusive.

This is the case for wild geese, but the situation is very different for reared grey geese. These grey geese cannot fly like the wild geese since they are bred in cages for another purpose. One day, a group of wild geese fly over the area and settle just one hundred metres from the grey geese. Then, something incredible happens. The wild geese begin to communicate with the tame geese. They fly over their cages and cry down to the others to follow them. The tame geese cannot. They try all they can to follow the wild geese, flapping their wings, honking back to them and running round to get air under their wings. But nothing happens. They simply cannot take off. The lady who owns the tame geese, can't stand this sorry spectacle, and opens her barn to the grey geese. This way, her tame geese can only hear their cries and not be teased by them flying above their heads.

The analogy to our situation in the silo is that we have lost our ability to fly. Our goal has changed. Perhaps one can say that we have got lazy, or fallen asleep in our enclosures. We no longer believe in ourselves, and we are satisfied by doing what is expected of us. It is high time that we looked up and learnt from the wild geese. Contrary to the tame geese, we are fully able to take responsibility for ourselves and our surroundings.

For now, we can summarise the following qualities which characterize leadership on the platform. The leader must:
- decide on the superordinate goal which can engage everyone and which can only be achieved when everyone plays their part.
- articulate the purpose and meaning of the company and what it is designed to do.
- create an understanding for serving the whole.
- equip the employees to achieve the maximum of personal leadership.
- create a framework with space and freedom for making one's own decisions without dominating or controlling those of others.
- keep the flow in terms of development and healthy growth.
- change the frame if it no longer serves the intention.

The philosophy behind the platform – *Summary*
- The employees are reliable, and seek responsibility and meaning in their work. They want to learn and solve problems for themselves. They have nothing against change, but offer resilience against being changed. They prefer to work than to be unemployed, and they want to be where they feel they can grow. Employees who meet openness and willing, will offer it in return.
- The best leaders lead because they believe in a cause, not because they seek power. Leaders driven by their cause are able to set superordinate goals and can ensure that there is always meaning behind what they do. They understand holistic systems and can create opportunity for

development via feedback and an empowerment towards their employees. The leaders create a framework with the space and freedom for making one's own decisions without dominating or controlling those of others. They can maintain the flow and change the frame if it no longer serves the intention.

- The best culture for an organisation builds on a holistic form of growth, connectivity and sustainability; flow, flex, and form.

AYNI – THE POWER OF RECIPROCITY

Of the five principles, ayni is the single most important concept of the Andean way. It is translated as reciprocity and means the interchange of loving, kindness, knowledge, and the fruits of one's labour between individuals, between humans and nature spirits. Reciprocity implies that one's labour is shared: I will help you today, and tomorrow you might help me. The purpose of reciprocity is the maintenance of life.

– The Shaman's Well

CHAPTER 6
The Power of Cohesion

What do the terms community, flexibility, exchange, relationship, reciprocity, mediation, facilitation, and cohesion have in common? They are all opposites of fragmentation. Fragmentation creates silos whilst cohesion and all the other terms create holistic platforms.

In January 2012, the UN General Secretary's Panel for Global Sustainability published a report which highlighted one of the most important causes to current problems; namely, our fragmented approach to global issues and the lack of cohesion between the different divisions whose duty it is to solve them. The world's next step of development is to create integrated solutions which serve the whole instead of only the parts. This chapter is about the forces which bind organisations and people together as a whole, and about what is required to strengthen cohesion on the new platforms.

Cohesion is a platform's life blood

Cohesion is also used today with respect to social capital; that is, the resources that are created as a result of regular human interaction. Such human relationships make us feel connected to something larger than ourselves. We feel that we are more than single pawns in the game, or cogs in the machine. Professor Robert D. Putnam of Harvard University considers cohesion or social capital to be determined by social network, trust, and norms. These three factors set up a symbiosis which makes it possible for people to create something larger than themselves through interaction. One also assesses how good a company is at *bonding* within its departments, *bridging* between departments, and *linking* between the leadership and the employees. It is also possible to measure a company's level of cohesion by counting the number of employees who consider the majority of people in the company to be, first of all, trustworthy and second, honest.

On the platform, it is not enough to focus only on the individual because synergy and therefore, added value, lies in the interaction between people and departments. As the pencil exercise showed, people need someone else to work with. As two or more, they then need to trust each other in order to *want* to share knowledge, insight, and experience. Finally, they need to be well-versed in a cooperative form of culture and behaviour based on information exchange, trust, and mutuality.

Ron Burt, Senior Researcher and Professor in Sociology at Chicago University, predicts that the ability to steer an organisation's social capital will be a core competence of the knowledge-based organisation. His reasoning builds on the premise that the more social capital there is, the better the relationships, and therefore, the greater the opportunity is to form strong alliances, partnerships, and joint ventures.

Social capital, both within a company and between companies, is a precondition for organisational learning, adaptability, and flexibility. Development then happens in the space between opposing poles or via *co-creation*, between synergetic or cooperative units.

We were already thinking along these lines 250 years ago, when people talked about *fraternity*, which is just another word for cohesion. Under the French Revolution, the revolutionary guard were joined in building a nation on *Liberté, Egalité, Fraternité* or freedom, equality, and fraternity. The introduction of freedom and equality raised no cause for doubt in Jacobean society, but fraternity led to problems, since it belonged to another sphere. Fraternity describes the moral duty one has to the group or community rather than individual rights of freedom and equality. Eventually though, all three spheres were accepted because there was a meeting of minds, combining individual values and rights (freedom and equality) with collective values (fraternity). Fraternity thus represented the realisation of a happy society without egoism and conflict. When we look at freedom, equality, and fraternity as a basis for society, this is a reminder that if we don't include cohesion then individualistic and egoistic drivers will stand alone. When compared to the terms flow, flex, and form, freedom corresponds to flow and growth, fraternity to flex, and cohesion and equality to form and sustainability. Without fraternity, and as such, without the link between growth and sustainability, we can't create sustainable growth.

It is necessary on the platform to create a new, independent, and structural unit whose purpose it is to promote and support cohesion and, in doing so, allow sustainable development and growth to be possible. With this in place, the company can prevent itself from falling back to a silo-based structure. A fragmentation of the organisation or a severing of employee relationships can be avoided. This new function can facilitate the pendulum's natural swing between order and chaos, and between centralised power and decentralised responsibility. This is crucial for the company's dynamic and adaptability and is often badly neglected by existing companies. All organisations operate with opposites and therefore are in need of a cohesive force that can enable flexibility and help to maintain a holistic focus. In the third section of this book, you can read more about how this new structural unit can be integrated within a company.

Personal responsibility to employees

The quality of leadership on the platform is vital, as is the quality of the employees and the effectiveness of its cohesive force. We know what motivates us as people but do we know what to look for in people when we invite them onto the platform and into our company?

The most important characteristics for allowing one to manoeuvre and navigate are freedom and responsibility.

Responsibility should be seen in relation to the framework set up by a company's purpose, means, and philosophy. An employee who is unwilling to support the mission used to set the company's framework, will not be able to form part of this framework or serve it effectively. A platform's leaders stays firm with regards to upholding the framework, but is open and empathetic with relation to his employees. If the framework isn't recognised by the employees and passed onto others, then its DNA will start to fade and eventually disappear. We will find ourselves in chaos, without purpose, or philosophy. Those people who cannot accept a company's superordinate goals or the conditions of its framework should not be invited onto the platform. Existing employees who have deviated should be realigned to the company framework, or, failing this, should be helped to make the shift to another framework and another company which will suit them better.

Besides staying loyal to the framework, the employees must also show loyalty to the person maintaining the framework and to their leader who uses it to drive daily business. The platform's employees are loyal and support their leader because their purpose and needs are the same. If the employee doesn't agree with their leader's way of setting up the framework, they can talk to a facilitator or to the department maintaining cohesion between the framework and the employees' activities. The employees who represent the activities carried out on the shop floor, have been involved in selecting their leader. Therefore they have the responsibility of supporting their judgments; just like the wild geese who cry out in support of the one flying in front and pulling the most weight. In this way, leadership is not a lonely and heavy job, but instead becomes a collective task based on solidarity and support.

In connection with his departure from the Danish bank, Danske Bank, former director Peter Straarup was asked by a journalist whether he considered his salary to be unusually high. Straarup looked directly into the camera and replied, "Not if you consider that I have given my life to Danske Bank." It was a potent moment. His wife remarked, "The bank has eaten up his life."

The question is how many people will give their lives without anyone in their flock crying out, and without the chance of another taking their position upfront, so that they can rest and avoid burn out. A revolving leadership would mean that people have the option to create a better work-life balance in certain periods of their life. This can benefit the organisation in that the leadership, at any one time, can reflect the specific kind of steer which the situation demands. After all, different situations call for different competences.

Decentralisation and the capital of trust

Nobel prize winning economist, Professor Joseph Stiglitz has, in recent years, travelled the world to explain how the price of inequality is putting the planet's very existence at risk. In an interview with Der Spiegel from October 2012, Stiglitz describes how "The American Dream" is a myth today, losing all relevance as the difference between rich and poor has become far too big. He expands on this point in an article for Vanity Fair and in his book, *The Price of Inequality*, in which he explains how one percent of the American population controls 40 percent of the nation's assets. But the future for the one percent is inextricably dependent on how the remaining 99 percent live their lives. If the 99 percent don't have adequate access to education or healthcare or receive some form of economic support, then in the long run, the problems encountered by the 99 percent will turn into problems for the one percent. These conditions are linked, but in American society, cohesion in terms of social capital is very low since there is too big a difference between rich and poor.

A tool which can be used to measure the level of cohesion in society is the Gini coefficient. A Gini coefficient can vary between zero and one. Zero corresponds to total equality and one to total inequality. A number closer to zero than one means good equality. This means that there can be a good exchange of knowledge between the top and bottom of the society, and indicates that the members of this society are trusting of the information they receive. In this way, there is less need for control and there is close contact between governance and activities being implemented. All circumstances can potentially be of benefit to the economy and to business. As Stiglitz writes in his book: "A focus on everyone's interests, or in other words, a focus on common welfare, is ultimately a precondition for one's own welfare. This is not only good for the soul. It is good for business."

According to Stiglitz, it is critical for a nation's competitiveness to have a low Gini coefficient. Scandinavia has a Gini coefficient of under 0.29, which is the lowest in the world. In comparison, the USA's Gini coefficient increased from 0.40 to 0.45 between 1997 and 2007 according to figures from the CIA's World Factbook, putting USA on the same level as Uganda.

The low Gini coefficient that we have in Scandinavia can be an important and determining factor when we want to create flexible, decentralised, and fast-responding organisations. If we want to create platforms with cohesion, then, according to Stiglitz, businesses need to play their part in supporting a political system that can maintain a low Gini coefficient. In this respect, the Nordic countries have a huge advantage. It is not enough for government to try to ensure a low Gini coefficient. Companies must also take responsibility for implementing a decentralised structure and pushing power and income downwards. Some people are probably horrified by the thought of decentralisation, but as you can read in the interviews with both Handelsbanken (page 45) and SAS (page 25), this was actually the key to their successes. If power stays at the top, the Nordic spirit disappears and it is much harder to uphold the competitiveness we can achieve by being the best at working together.

Many people in the Nordic countries have difficulty in working in top-down American organisations because they experience that they use, what should be, productive time filling out reports rather than actually getting the job done. When trust is absent, the power of control increases. This trend is coming to Scandinavia too, so if we aren't careful we could end up with control, mistrust, and heavily, bureaucratic organisations. This would be a situation raising costs and wasting us time, without giving any clear benefit when trust is already built into the system. As Wallander from Handelsbanken says, it is more difficult to decentralise than to centralise. Centralisation happens almost on its own since power and control run so deep in so many organisations. Decentralisation, on the other hand, demands conscious actions and focus together with a leadership who considers it a primary task of theirs, to push towards decentralisation. This must be done, despite a typical result being that they end up losing power and influence for themselves and can even risk making themselves surplus to requirements. To lead on the new platform, demands a great self-awareness and great self-insight. As such, it is often best to let the team of a decentralised organisation choose a leader for themselves, with the board of directors as the highest layer, having already designed the framework by agreeing on the purpose, means, and philosophy.

The power of cohesion – *Summary*

– A culture and behaviour of cooperation demands information, trust, and mutuality.
– An organisation's social capital is a core competence on the new platform since it creates better relationships in and between companies, and at the same time, is a precondition for organisational learning, adaptability and flexibility.
– We need a mediating connection between growth and sustainability in order to ensure cohesion.
– Information, trust and mutuality, are vital elements on the new platform. For them to prosper, we need to decentralise power and responsibility.

3-DIMENSIONAL

"A happy and coordinated new millenium to you all. Our gracious Circle of High Circles wishes you all another year of productive employment serving the Ministry of Regularity, His Roundness, Pantocyclus hereby bestows the following proclamations: Every new millennium, the State has been troubled by ill-intentioned persons pretending to have received revelations from another world, a third dimension. Such a notion is of course absurd and furthermore illegal."

– Edwin A. Abbott, in the book *Flatland*

"Our Age of Anxiety is, in great part, the result of trying to do today's jobs with yesterday's tools!"

– Marshall McLuhan, Canadian Philosopher

CHAPTER 7

The tools we'll need

As the quotation from the book, *Flatland*, illustrates, it can be difficult to see the *new* when we look with *old* eyes. Sometimes the new can even seem absurd. Many people have great difficulty in adjusting to something when they cannot yet see how it's going to affect them. This is how we perceive the holistic system; that is, we don't fully see it or believe in it because we are much more used to only seeing its parts, divisions, and departments. But we get no useful information by delving into detail because the reality we are working in is much bigger than the individual elements.

As such, we must bid farewell to certain tools since they no longer serve us or our companies. This applies, for example, to budgets and organisation diagrams. You can also disregard the left half of your brain and all control strategies. Instead, you can benefit from using, amongst other things, bench-marking, the right half of your brain, and storytelling.

This chapter will not cover all new methods and tools which will be needed on the new platform, but it will offer insight into the most important. In addition, you will be given more knowledge on the philosophy behind the platform.

When the map no longer shows landscape
We have left the mechanical silo mindset, which assumes that the whole can be understood by only describing the parts. Nature and the function of its organisms cannot be explained by only analysing its components. We know, therefore, that the three crises are linked: the economic crisis, with its lack of capital and new markets; the eco-

logical crisis, with the attack on nature; and the energy crisis, with the depletion of raw materials. They all originate because our fragmented systems don't give us the opportunity to think long-term or to think holistically. We are lacking the necessary information to act as an intelligent, cohesive species.

To truly understand the potential of holism and cohesion, then we need only look at quantum physics.

Physicians have now proven that nothing can exist at an atomic level without being in relation to something else. This is why we don't operate with fragments and restrictions on the platform. Instead, we deal with opportunities and remain open to what is going on around us, observing without judging so that we might establish new patterns.

If we want to discover a new pattern, the tool to use is no longer the left half of our brain, well-tuned to deal with the rational and operational yet only in two dimensions, as fragments, single units and numbers. Instead, we should engage the right half of our brain which is primarily intuitive and conceptual and can read and create in three-dimensions and holistically. Our starting point for creating the new must also be new, so that we don't fall back to organisation diagrams, budgets, and accounts, which will be useless to us when plotting our future. When we leave one mindset behind, the tools we used in the silos can no longer be used. We need another joystick to steer us.

Niels Bohr presented what is best known as the Copenhagen version of quantum theory. According to him, a particle is what one can measure it to be. Quantum physics is also called "the physics of possibilities". Bohr explained that nature likes to keep its options open and, as such, it is able to follow every possible path. When we observe something that looks like a wave, it's a wave. When we observe something that looks like a particle, it's a particle. When we attempt to measure a fragment, whether a company's economy or an individual's performance, what we see is a picture of the reality that reflects how we observe and measure it. This means that we miss all the possibilities that can otherwise be found in the system. We end with a two-dimensional reality instead of looking for the three-dimensional. But the better we get at staying open and in keeping searching, the greater the possibility we have of finding the golden nugget that lies between the elements. As a Sufi master once said: "You think that because two *and* two make four, you understand, but you must also understand the *and*." The mechanisms which focus on measuring, steering, or controlling fragments either measure the "two" or the result, "four". They don't measure what lies between and therefore, they won't work on the platform, where cohesion is just as important a part of the whole as the separate elements are.

What we need is a new tool-box that can help us see the whole picture which currently hides out of sight. If we thought that our world was only made in two-dimensions, as described by Edwin Abbott in *Flatland*, and that people were geometric figures like circles, lines, and triangles, we wouldn't have the knowhow to measure the third dimension. When this world is visited by a spherical object its people didn't know what to do; just as 500 years ago, we didn't know how to navigate the world's oceans. On our map of the seas, the world was flat, not round. This is why it is necessary for us to find new navigation tools that we can employ on the landscapes of our three-dimensional platforms.

Emergence: When the whole is more important than the separate parts

The term emergence means to open outwards, to come forward, to bloom. It can also be used to describe the particular characteristics appearing from a holistic system, when these cannot be described as only separate elements.

According to the theory of emergence, certain characteristics first come about when an organism is sufficiently developed and complex. One talks about processes of synergy, where interaction creates either more or something else than the individual components. What emerges is a characteristic that does not individually belong to any of the components of the system, yet belongs to the system itself. In the same way as we didn't know that adding two hydrogen molecules to a molecule of oxygen would result in a liquid we now know as water.

We can first observe what is new when this is present and visible. We couldn't have predicted it if it didn't resemble the components we started out with. We couldn't have set up a budget or devised a strategy for achieving the final characteristics. This means that the way we used to make strategies can no longer work for us. We navigate from an old map, on which sustainable growth doesn't exist, only growth. In 1979, a well-respected strategist of the time, George Steiner, wrote in his book, *"Strategic Planning; What every manager must know"* that: "To be successfully implemented, every strategy must be broken down into its constituent parts." But instead of breaking things down into lesser components, emergence makes it possible for us to understand the bigger picture. It allows us to store our experiences and through this develop new thinking and new commercial opportunities.

Working with emergence theory on the platform demands, as mentioned earlier, that the framework and superordinate goal is clearly defined by the leadership and that there is ample space and freedom for the employees to develop. What is also needed is an internal dialogue system in which facilitators, in collaboration with the employees, can check whether the means of reaching the goal are working effectively and what is emerging along the way. For this to happen, the organisation needs to be sufficiently open and tolerant and there needs to be trust between people and the organisation.

From feedback to debriefing

"Our companies have become too big to fail," is something we hear often in business circles. One could just as well add, "Too big to fail, too big to change."

According to emergence theory, systems can become so strong that it is impossible to change them. Once things are born, they take on their own life and cannot be changed by going back and retracing the steps. You can read more about this in leadership guru, Margaret Wheatley's book, *"So Far From Home,"* in which she describes new systems created with emergence as holding a power and influence which far exceeds the sum of the individual elements. The new systems will have qualifications and competences which weren't present in the original local parts or elements and these will always surprise us. There is a strength in nature which is far beyond our current comprehension. The biologists, Humberto Maturana and Franciso Varela operate on the basis that you can't impose control a living system, you can only disturb it. Therefore, we should ensure that the companies on our platforms don't get too big and that we are given constant feedback with regards to what and how things are developing.

Feedback will, by virtue of its nature, describe what has already happened or what has already shown itself as emergence. We cannot observe what hasn't yet emerged. Furthermore, Maturana and Varela suggest that our brains have difficulty in accepting new information. 80 percent of the information we use to evaluate something or create something new, is taken from the information we already have stored in the brain. Less than 20 percent is taken in from outside. This means that changes are much more likely to occur from the inside out rather than from the outside in, where other people can influence how we think and act. This insight also puts *command and control systems* in perspective since we have an inborn resistance to changes that are forced upon on us externally and tell us what to do. If, on the other hand, changes originate from within ourselves, they can be implemented faster and more sustainably since they are aligned to our own beliefs.

Feedback which arrives externally, either as positive or negative, is not of too much interest or relevance in our explorations here. We are familiar with the so-called *sandwich model* where we issue or receive positive feedback first, then negative and finally, more positive. Packaging the negative feedback between two pieces of positive, makes it easier to communicate and easier to receive feedback from others.

What we are interested in, is a kind of *feedforward* model where we focus on what works. If we put our focus on what the individual elements are doing wrong then we lose our overview of the whole. Mistakes are a key part of learning and development. As the former CEO of NOVO Nordisk, Mads Øvilsen, has said: "If you don't make atleast three mistakes per day, you make too few." The feedforward we need is the kind of information that is present in the system, but which isn't directly visible or measurable since we are not yet aware that it exists. It isn't of particular interest whether feedback is positive or negative because this doesn't help us to determine which way the system is swaying and whether it is moving towards out overriding goal.

On a platform, we can observe what is happening in the system and not whether this is right or wrong. That which is right for one system can well be wrong for another. What is of more interest is to keep track of what is working in bringing the company closer to its overriding goal, and what isn't, so that the latter can be realigned or extinguished before it has the chance to get so far that it can no longer be changed.

In the area of national defense, there has been great success in using debriefing as a method of reporting the events that have happened out in the field. A regiment's leader will hold a series of meetings to collect information from different troops as they return home after a mission. Every soldier is encouraged to contribute their own version of events in order to form a bigger and more accurate picture of what happened so that this can then be presented to all members of the team. This happens to enable learning, similar to the way nature employs trial-and-error processes in order to test what works best. The system allows whatever works to continue, but whatever fails is stopped and an alternative action is attempted instead.

Debriefing is based on the understanding that an organism functions holistically. It wouldn't make sense to assess a situation based on the experience of only one soldier. This appears in stark contrast to traditional feedback, which operates relative to good and bad, or right and wrong. Debriefing contains no evaluation or judgement, only observation and learning in terms of what can be put to future use.

Debriefing is *not*:
- a session held under stressful conditions
- a session held only with individuals
- a scoping of negative feelings
- an evaluation or critique, regardless of whether learning is to be gained
- a scoping exercise to reveal a scapegoat and attribute blame

Debriefing *is* a method that makes it possible to:
- identify experience which can be used in the future
- create a common picture of what happened
- avoid frustration and stress by helping the team to position the experience in a common context which can then be treated
- highlight what works in the system
- reduce the feeling of isolation
- increase the level of belonging and collective spirit

Ernesto Yturralde from Equador, who researches and facilitates debriefing processes with professor Peter Senge from MIT, explains: "With regards to experience-based learning methods, debriefing is a semi-structured process. Once a particular activity is complete, the facilitator will pose a series of questions progressively and at the appropriate point in the session. This allows the participants to explain what has happened and pass on important knowledge that can be used for future activities. This allows us to connect the initial challenge with the resultant learning and with the future."

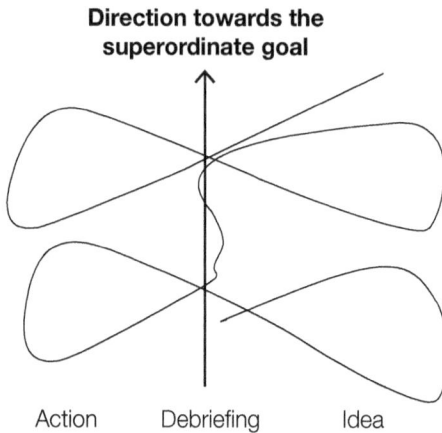

Direction towards the superordinate goal

Action   Debriefing   Idea

When debriefing is used as a tool on the platform, then the company can build up a collective intelligence and knowledge which can be used to navigate the platform forwards. This can both be knowledge that can be used again, or knowledge which should no longer be used at all. Without misunderstanding this as static or statutory *best practice,* debriefing allows us to establish what works best, here and now, and how it can inspire others in the system. (read also the interview with Jan Wallander from Handelsbanken on page 45).

Debriefing gives us the chance to observe how an intention or idea develops once it is released to the outside world. Like the trial-and-error processes of nature, debriefing enables us to learn from what happened last time, alter the process and then run the idea again to check, via a subsequent debriefing, whether things work better. *Figure 9* shows the interaction that occurs between idea and implementation in a debriefing culture and how this interaction constantly ensures that one can keep moving towards the overriding goal by incorporating any emergence along the way. This is sustainable growth.

From organisation diagrams to web organisms

A tool paramount in silos is the organisation diagram. It shows which boxes the different employees belong in, thus allowing them (and their customers) to orient themselves. The intention is that each box contains different functions which the employees are assigned to do, meaning that we can attach names and titles to them. There are, for example, HR, CSR, communication, IT, economy, logistics, law, production etc. We divide things up in order to understand them, but we do this without considering that we are lacking cohesion. As such, there is little chance that any form of holistic environment will be able to emerge. The organisation diagram reflects our need to create comfort by explaining details.

Scientific research to discover the most basic matter and building blocks of our existence have led to the realisation that there are none. The deeper physicists probe into nature, the more they must acknowledge that the only thing they find are relationships. Physicists describe neutrons and electrons as "a set of relations, which can reach outwards to other things." Despite allotting different names to them, these particles are not always visible until they are positioned in relation to other particles. Everything in the universe is made up of these *"bundles of potential"* only manifest their potential via relations. Recent brain research reaches the same conclusion. Nothing exists without the other. We are social creatures and our brains are social organisms. We are connected to each other, and no project is an individual project.

We live in a culture that doesn't recognise this fact of science. This is why we still put people in boxes instead of turning our focus on the relationship and the potential in the relationship. We draw organisation diagrams with lines that connect the silos and rely on reports and predefined channels of communication. But our neatly drawn diagrams are just as fictitious as the building blocks are for the physicists. The only form of organisation used by nature are networks

of internally connected, and mutually dependent relationships. This also applies to human organisations. The organisation diagram, its figures, and its lines, are imaginary. The
real organisation is always a close network of relationships.

When we operate from a platform, we must find a means
of maintaining a full perspective of the whole. We need to go
from a two-dimensional organisation diagram to a three-dimensional organisation network, or a so-called *"hologram"*.
The hologram gives a real and beautiful representation of
the organisation, which you can read about in the interview
with Novo Nordisk on page 173. Handelsbanken doesn't
have an organisation diagram, since they consider themselves to be a network and not a hierarchy.

As Wallander says: "If you want to find someone, then
look in the internal telephone book." (see his interview on
page 45). Hierarchy will remove the dynamic and flow from
an organisation which sees itself as an organism, and can
only work as a whole.

Since the power in a hierarchy is positioned at the top, an organisation diagram will expose graphically how one loses power towards the bottom of the diagram. Many people fight to get as high up in the pyramid as possible. Handelsbanken describes itself as an organism consisting of three circles: in the middle are the *branch offices*; in the next circle, the *regions*; and in the last and outer most circle, the *central office* (see fig. 10). The branch offices' tasks are the most important as it is they who have closest contact to the customer. They know best what the customer needs, which is precisely what creates income for the business. The branch offices are the heart of the organisation. The job of the regions is to visit the branch offices and listen to what they need. The job of central office is to serve the needs and wishes of the branch offices, which have been established and passed on to them by the regions. The regions function as facilitators, creating cohesion between the branch offices and central office. The job of central office is to set up the framework that can lift the entire company towards its goal.

Demand stems from the inside out, or from bottom to top, that is; from the branch offices to central office. There is no push top-down or outside-in. The central circle's task (ie. the branch offices' task), is to function as the direct contact to the customers. The task of the other two circles is to serve the inner circle. This way of organising is the lifeblood of Handelsbanken and of decentralisation, where all power and influence is closest to the customers. Since the branch offices know what works and what doesn't, it is this body which implements the core idea of the company. The branch offices can demand anything which supports the overriding goal.

We have talked about how a good leader will set up a strong framework in order to keep heading towards a company's superordinate or overriding goal. Another word for framework, is the term, *context*. The leadership works with the *context*, whilst the employees work with the *content*.

The role of leadership is to ensure that the content can have the best conditions for development within its context. The leadership must take great care in serving its content. If a context doesn't have content, then it will resemble a soap bubble that pops with the slightest touch. It lacks the substance and resistance that can only be built from the inside-out. If the content has no context, then it will disappear like water without a container. Thus, leadership and employees work symbiotically.

A platform's organisation reflects the dynamic that exists between the context and the content. In the case of Handelsbanken, the regions provide cohesion such that the context and the content function as one entity. No one of the three functions is more important than the other. As such, none can be eliminated. It is not particular significant for the employees *where* they are placed, since no function carries a higher status than another.

The organisation's resilience

A system can have a high or low level of resilience. In the silos, the strength of a company is measured in terms of its stability. One measures equity relative to balance to see how economically stable a company is. On a platform, a company's resilience can be described in terms of its flexibility and adaptability, and how many versions of itself it can maintain at the same time. These are all characteristics supported by a decentralised system.

In the world of physics, resilience is defined as the physical characteristic that makes it possible for a material to return to its original form or position after undergoing a change that doesn't exceed the materials elastic limits or resistance. Some systems, companies, or people, have a high degree of resilience and will recover stronger from something that may cause others to crack. Those with a high resilience can learn new skills as they struggle onwards, which they can then implement and use to their advantage; for example, a debriefing process. These people can create new and better alternatives of what no longer works. Those with low resilience break down and cannot manage to get through the dark hole which a crisis or transformation often entails. Some times we need to hit rock bottom and feel it under our feet before we can establish a new approach. This process demands resilience and adaptability.

In the article, *"The Nordic Way,"* which was issued by the Nordic Council of Ministers in connection with the World Economic Forum in Davos in 2011, the Nordic territories were described as having a high level of resilience. Justification for this was that Sweden, Finland, Norway and Denmark had braved the economic crisis well, adjusting quickly to the new conditions. According to the article's authors, this resilience is due to the Scandinavian countries' small size, open economies and high income per capita. All Nordic countries have a large public sector and demand high taxes. All have an infrastructure that supports common well-being. A high level of cohesion and a low Gini coefficient are also consequences of these factors, so too is the decentralised system in which many people take responsibility for the whole and adjust quickly to new situations.

As mentioned, Handelsbanken is one of the best examples of a decentralised model that has been successfully implemented. Their CEO at the time, Arne Mårtensson, wrote the following about Handelsbanken's decentralised structure in the company's year report of 2000: "Handelsbanken's consistently high performance with regards to cost-cutting is primarily due to the structure of our organisation. The bank has, over many years, developed a non-hierarchical network organisation in which different departments have a great deal of responsibility and self-sufficiency, both in terms of administration and commercial leeway. This means that they are in the best position to serve the customer. A very flat organisation, with only three functional areas, operates via an inner market which has removed all hierarchical decision making. If there is no demand for a certain product, then it will automatically disappear. The glue that holds the organisation together is a very strong company culture. In the new economy, flat network organisations will become common practice. Handelsbanken has an advantage here. We have, for many years, been streamlining this way of working and it has afforded us great competitiveness. Our experience is that it takes a long time to yield all the advantages of this type of organisation. It needs to be done gradually in order to get the control mechanisms to work properly, and the organisation to mature."

A system's resilience is determined both by the characteristics of the people in the system and by the structure of the system in which they operate. Therefore, it isn't enough for the leadership to take a top-down decision to change a centralised culture to a decentralised culture without having made sure that all employees have understood the reason for the change and are ready to share responsibility for taking this course. When leadership decides that the organisation will, from now on, operate on a decentralised platform, one needs to facilitate the employees into taking their place in the framework. This requires the company to mature and shift its culture, which clearly cannot happen from one day to the next. It is in this light that Arne Mårtensson's words should be reflected on. Cultural change takes time, patience, and constant focus. A leader who begins to express doubt in the middle of the transformation process can do more harm than good, since they have left one system but have not yet set foot on the new platform. The employees are left in the middle of crossing the river (see the interview with Michael Møllmann from Novo Nordisk on page 173). The leadership must continuously hold onto the new framework in order for cultural change to happen and allow the new decentralised structure to become reality.

Another example of how a decentralised system offers more resilience than a hierarchical system is Spain's landing in Central America. In 1519, Hernán Cortés led a few hundred Spanish in battle against several thousand natives to destroy the Aztec Capital, Tenochtitlán, which was, at the time, the centre point of the largest empire in Central America. In so doing, Cortés conquered Mexico. In the two years that followed, he succeeded in dissolving a thousand-year-old Aztec empire, under emperor Moctezuma the Second, and his successor, Cuauhtémoc. Thus, Cortés paved the way for Spanish colonial power to spread across the whole territory.

Later, the Spanish repeated their success, this time with commander Francisco Pizzarro, who overthrew the Inca Empire in 1532 by executing the ruler of the Incas, Atahualpa, after just one year's battle, and positioning a puppet ruler in his place.

In 1680 the Spanish went to war again. This time against the Apache civilization by attacking and seizing their territory. However, the Spanish didn't succeed in beating the Apache for the next 200 years! What was their secret? It is the same secret that we have discussed throughout this book, and which is also the secret of a resilient system: Decentralisation.

When centralising, one becomes vulnerable and easy to hit, because power and knowledge are not distributed throughout the system as a whole. Without several pathways to choose towards the same vision, one begins to lose diversity and creativity. As such, one begins to lose cohesion and struggles to keep momentum in one's activities. Both the Aztec and Inca kingdoms were formed as very hierarchical, pyramid-like structures with one person ruling at the very top. When the Spanish wanted to overthrow the kingdom, they just beheaded the leader and took the throne and thus, the entire kingdom for themselves. Very simple.

In a decentralised structure, it is much more difficult to figure out where to go to find a higher concentration of power. In actual fact, there is no such concentration. Power is distributed to everyone in the structure. The more Apaches that the Spanish killed, the more this raised the level of cohesion and togetherness amongst those left standing. Each tribe was supported by the framework and the superordinate goal that justified their existence. This was facilitated by the medicine man, Nant'an, who had no power over others, but who lived and breathed the spirit of the tribe. The most well-known Nant'an is Geronimo, whose tribe followed him voluntarily since the word "must" does not exist in the Apache language.

Resilience is the cohesive force that enables a system to shift and adapt itself whilst under attack or when challenged by crisis. When a decentralised system has a higher resilience than a hierarchical system, then it would be logical to introduce a new Gini tool for companies to keep track of how decentralised the structure has become, to what extent power is evenly distributed, and to maintain a salary structure in which the difference between CEO salaries and employee salaries didn't become too great. This could be called the *Geronimo coefficient*, after the Apache who inspired an entire tribe to follow him voluntarily by clearly expressing a vision for the good of the company, rather than merely for his own gain.

There are several reasons to introduce a Geronimo coefficient in an organisation. On one level, the company demonstrates that they share responsibility for maintaining a low Gini coefficient, thus improving the competitive position. On another level, top leadership show that they act as a collective entity, in which all elements are important and where their own salaries are not disproportionally higher than an average employee's. Finally, the leadership show that shifts within the leadership, which result in a leader joining another part of the organisation will not have an especially drastic impact on the work or welfare of that person.

By allowing the Geronimo coefficient to form an integral part of the company's public accounts, those companies with a low coefficient send a clear message to the market that they function as a collective and that top leadership is able to undergo change. The company demonstrates its resilience. It won't just fall if the head gets toppled as was the case for the Aztec and Inca empires.

Trash budgets and use benchmarking

On our platform, we will wave goodbye to budgets. Wallander chose to remove the control function and all budgetting at Handelsbanken. When the goal is relative, there is no reason in pinpointing it with exact numbers. Such measured forecasting creates no real value and attempts to predict a future we don't know. It is relationships that can best show how things are at any particular moment, dependent on one's own, and others' behaviour.

The way that Handelsbanken determines whether they have achieved their goal and done their work well, is to *benchmark* themselves against their competitors and their respective accounts. The term *benchmarking* probably didn't exist thirty years ago when Wallander was developing his model. Today, we understand *benchmarking* as a comparison of commercial processes against best practice from other businesses or industries. Handelsbanken's CEO in 2001, Lars O. Grönstedt, wrote the following about replacing budgets with *benchmarking* in the yearly report: "The person who is responsible (for a particular task) should be able to compare their performance, not against something as abstract as a plan or budget, but against something as tangible as, for example, the results achieved by someone in a similar position and over the same period. This is why *benchmarking* is an important instrument for Handelsbanken. We have survived just fine without budgets for thirty years."

The time spent and the frustration generated in filling out budgets and forecasting the future can be turned into a significant saving in costs. In this respect, the companies operating on platforms already have a competitive edge when *benchmarking* themselves against other companies who use time and money on budgets and control.

Which half of the brain do we need to employ?

Nature has equipped us with two halves to our brains, connected internally via our *corpus callosum,* which, just like a facilitator, enables information to be exchanged between the two halves.

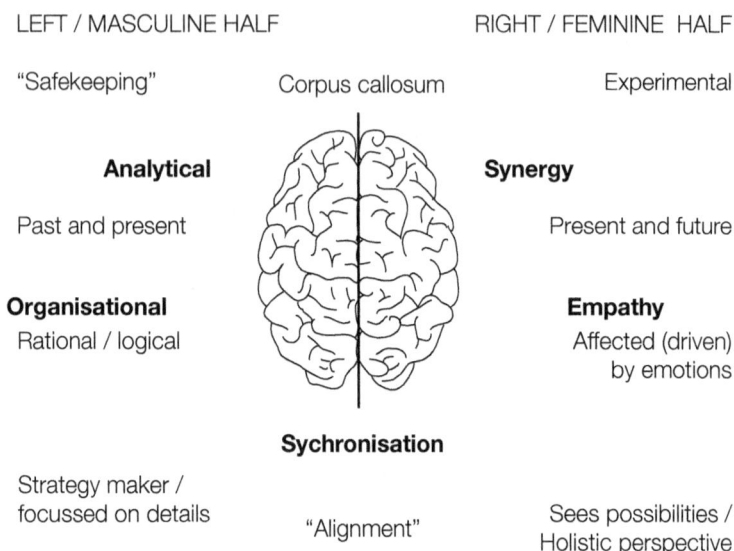

LEFT / MASCULINE HALF		RIGHT / FEMININE HALF
"Safekeeping"	Corpus callosum	Experimental
Analytical		**Synergy**
Past and present		Present and future
Organisational		**Empathy**
Rational / logical		Affected (driven) by emotions
	Sychronisation	
Strategy maker / focussed on details	"Alignment"	Sees possibilities / Holistic perspective

The left half of our brain is mostly concerned with the rational, logistical, and analytical, whilst the right half of the brain concerns itself with concepts and holism (see fig. 11). The right half receives images and is supported by one's experience. All senses and feelings work together. The processes occur together and can spread themselves in all directions, so that one can have several images "on screen" at the same time. In this way one can establish a quick overview. Thinking in pictures happens very quickly and partly unconciously. It is a creative, intuitive, and holistic way to think. In the last few years, there has been great focus on our brains, and how we use them. For many years, we have primarily used the left side of our brains to lead our companies.

On the new platforms, we will need to make better use of the right half of our brains. The right side will serve us best since it is best equipped to work with the whole, with concepts, and with possibilities. Platform companies support and create space for this way of thinking by eliminating budgets, organisation diagrams, and evaluation feedback, which rather belong to the left side of the brain. As a platform-based company, you will need to invest energy in developing your employees' emotional and social intelligence so that they can better understand their customers and their needs.

In his book, *"A Whole New Mind – Why Right-Brainers Will Rule the Future,"* Daniel Pink describes how a new way for us to exist will demand completely new ways to think. Pink names the time we are living in as *The Conceptual Age.* When we use the right half of our brain, we can develop, design, tell stories, play, and create symphony and meaning. All characteristics help shape a company's *blue ocean* strategy, which, by definition, is a conceptual business model that runs against typical business models. One example, as mentioned earlier, is Cirque du Soleil, which combines ballet, opera, and circus, in synergy. The result is a unique product which, as yet, has no competition. A second example is Apple, a third is Nike, and there are many more.

However, we still see a major problem for organisations and companies locked in structures that were developed for, and worked very well in, an industrial society, but which don't function in the fast-changing world we now live in.

The rational and logical left half of the brain cannot develop platforms. We need to go beyond only thinking in linear terms, moving directly from A to B, from past to present, in progressive sequence, or in boxes. The left half of the brain devises the strategy which is fastest, best, and cheapest. But we need to shake ourselves up and reshape ourselves as a conceptual society. We will begin to see new structures for employees, so that each can reach their full potentials. They need to be given the responsibility, power, and freedom to think outside the box. The right half of their brains will perhaps be their most important working tool in shaping value and emergence, and thus, sustainable growth.

The force of history

According to Roger Schank, Yale Professor in computer technology and psychology, people are created to understand stories. They are not created to understand logic. A story has its own force, not only as entertainment, but as a means of conveying knowledge and intelligence. When a company uses storytelling, and the same story is heard over and over again, this creates a force of cohesion on the platform. It helps to create common identity and direction. A good story is holistic. It can encapsulate the feelings that a spreadsheet of accounts or budgets can never express. When we have understood the essence of a story, we don't need detailed instructions to navigate or to know what is expected of us. It is critical that we develop our ability to create common images in the form of stories that the entire company and the world around us can relate to.

In February 2012, *Forbes* magazine ran a competition for the best business story. The motivation for this was that the entrepreneurs who had formed emotional ties with their employees, investors, and customers were shown to achieve greater, longer-lasting gains in capital if they had also managed to tell meaningful stories about their businesses. The company selected as winner was IKEA. Their story is strong and is written clearly on their website:

"Beautifully designed household products are usually made for the few people who can afford them. From the beginning, IKEA has chosen another strategy. We have decided to stand on the side of the many. This means that we meet the needs for home furnishing products all over the world: for people with very different tastes and very different needs, dreams, hopes and incomes – people who want to improve their home and their everyday life." From IKEA website (2013).

Every company has a destiny-creating story which is a big part of its identity. Whether a company was started in a basement or on a polished floor, the memory matters. It matters that a company has lived through experiences that have changed the company's culture; these all form part of its common story and identity, which should continue to be told. Not least, in order to give a hint of how the next chapter in history will unfold.

Use five minutes to tell your version of your company's story. Does this make you proud and happy?

Rituals are a good excuse for celebrating life

A part of a company's story is its traditions or rituals. It is a basic human need to mark the phases in one's life. There is a reason why we celebrate birthdays and anniversaries and carry out the different riutals that our religions or traditions oblige. The expression "Rites of Passage" is sometimes used for the rituals which mark a transition from one phase in a person's life to the next.

A ritual or ceremony is also a way to honour someone who has contributed to a company's or a society's welfare. In silos, people would primarily be rewarded in the form of a higher salary, new car, or other material good, as evidence that they are important for the company. We must find other ways to show that we honour these people and are grateful for what they have done for the company and the local community. Their input is a part of the company's common story. When we visit provincial towns across a country, we see statues of the citizens that did something important for their town. It can be the person who opened the first sawmill, saved someone's life or brought electricity to the area. The town and its residents want to show their gratitude to these people.

In 1900, the symbolist artist, George Frederic Watts, took the initiative to create a memorial wall at the Postman's Park in London. This was to commemorate all the people who had risked their lives or given their lives for the sake of others.

Honouring people who have done something extraordinary for the company happens at all levels and follows all kinds of tasks. Gratitude, and recognition have much more value to us than money, and they are a lot more motivating. In silos, one's salary and position in the hierarchy is the decisive factor for getting recognition and respect. Therefore, everyone fights to get the highest position and the highest salary. On a platform though, all elements are important in order for the group to function. Those who give more to the group, get more recognition and respect. The time is ripe to let the movement free! You can read more about this in the third section of the book.

The tools we need – *Summary*
- Network organisations, without hierarchy, boxes, and organisation diagrams.
- *Benchmarking*, where budgets are trashed and replaced by us forming comparisons.
- *Debriefing*, where the holistic system's feedback is most important.
- Resilience as measured by a new *Geronimo coefficient* for the company, as opposed to the *Gini coefficient* for a nation.
- The power of the right half of the brain to see holistically and in patterns.
- Storytelling, to create common identity, pride and purpose.
- Rituals and celebration.

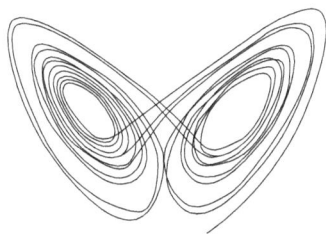

Part III: SET THE MOVEMENT FREE

"We know that all problems have complex causes.
We do not place blame on any one person or cause,
including ourselves and our colleagues."

– Margaret Wheatley

"The caterpillar body holds us to where we were,
and it holds the impulse of a better world;
of what we could become."

– Barbara Marx Hubbard

THE NATURAL WORLD

"We must draw our standards from the natural world. We must honour with the humility of the wise, the bounds of that natural world and the mystery which lies beyond, admitting that there is something in the order of being which evidently exceeds all our competence."

– Vaclav Havel

"Nature runs on sunlight.
Nature uses only the energy it needs.
Nature fits form to function.
Nature recycles everything.
Nature rewards cooperation.
Nature banks on diversity.
Nature demands local expertise.
Nature curbs excesses from within.
Nature taps the power of limits."

– Janine Benyus,
author of *"Biomimicry"*.

CHAPTER 8
The Movement

The first section of the book is about how rigid silo structures don't serve the dynamic company or the society that accommodates it. The second section of the book looks at the building blocks a company needs: the beliefs and tools needed to develop flexible and moveable platforms. In this third section, the different elements are put together to form a holistic leadership model taht can set employees and leadership free and thus, prepare them for the new platform.

In this chapter, we will see what a movement is and how it can set a company free. You will be given the basis for understanding how you and your company can benefit from the knowledge that exists in nature, for example, from swarms of specific species and continuous gaming. You will see the huge benefits that can be drawn from a movement, and will appreciate what it takes to set a movement free.

A company in perpetual motion

"We cannot *run* a business. More than 25 years ago, we learnt that business must run itself. Responsibility creates results, not authority."

With these words, Bill Gore, founder of *Gore-Tex*, summarises the basic principle behind the movement that I propose. I define *movement* as a collective activity that is directed to cause wide-reaching change and achieve its goal either with or without collaboration with established organisations.

The *cooperative movement* is one of the best known examples we have in Denmark. It is a description of a specific company structure and the close economic cooperation struck between agriculture, fishing and horticulture. Denmark's cooperative movement should not only be understood as a special legal, economic, and organisational model. It has its roots in the agricultural structures and values of the late 19th century. The cooperative movement sits in people's consciousness as a characteristically Danish economic-democratic tradition, which justifies the Scandinavia and especially Denmark that we have ended up with today.

I would like to expand the term movement to include both internal and external relations on the platform. The driver of such a movement has its origin in a collective and shared responsibility amongst employees, for achieving a common goal through everyone contributing. There are already companies that exist as movements. One of them is California's fourth largest producer of tomato-based foods, *The Morning Star Company*. Morning Star has created a movement that is extremely well-synchronised; working as an organism and, at the same time, employing a completely decentralised operation. This movement requires that the leadership gives freedom, power, and responsibility back to the employees, and that the workforce is ready to accept power, and motivate themselves. As Morning Star say: "Other companies get leaders who cannot pass on their power, or employees who cannot accept power or responsibility for their lives and are therefore afraid to take responsibility for doing the tasks the company expects them to do."

A company that operates like a movement will focus on the employees and a decentralised responsibility structure. Employees are expected to make themselves and their work visible. Employees are expected to work well in cooperative processes with their colleagues. Just like in Morning Star, the work force on a platform must set their own individual goals for ensuring that their company achieves more together than it would with a set of unconnected individual contributions.

TOP-DOWN
Collective leadership

The company's
competence

The company's
structure and
organisation

INNER — THE NEW PLATFORM — OUTER

Your values and
beliefs

Your behaviour and
individual actions

BOTTOM-UP
The individual employees

Set the employees free

In the year 2011 to 2012, the *VELUX foundation* supported the future research bureau, *House of Futures*, in exploring what society could expect to happen over the next 100 years. In connection with a seminar focussing on how the future would be created and by whom, participants were asked to choose one of four fields which they considered most important on the above diagram (fig. 12). They could choose between an inner personal drive or an external one. At the same time, they could choose between a top-down or bottom-up perspective.

The participants were asked to mark the field in which they already worked, using a black dot. Before reading on, then consider the following questions:

1. Which of the four areas in figure 12 do you think will be the most important for creating a new business platform? (position your red dot)

2. In which of the four quarters do you work currently
   (position the black dot)

The majority of the participants at the future seminar placed their red dot in the quadrant, "inner-drive / bottom-up". They believed that the key changes towards a sustainable society would be driven by ourselves, internally and bottom-up. Despite the fact that most of us share this belief, today's current development is, in fact, steered, to a large extent, top-down and from the outside inwards. As proof of this, most of the seminar participants placed their black dots in the upper right quadrant. This can help explain why a transformation will be difficult to acheive if leaders don't give their employees the freedom they need within a new framework for decentralised decision making.

My belief is that the platform can be put in motion if leadership creates an external framework in the form of an overriding goal, and then releases their employees to navigate freely within this framework.

A movement cannot be ignited by top-down decisions alone since it relies on the energy created when the employees *feel* ownership and responsibility. Neither can a movement be started by only employing a bottom-up approach, since the common goal and direction for the movement won't have been articulated. A movement is initiated when top meets bottom, and external meets internal. It is in the dynamic and relation between these opposing poles that the platform exists.

A way to explain this is with the help of the zeroth law of thermodynamics, which concerns equilibrium. When two systems come in contact with each other then, unless they are in thermal equlibrium, there will be a transfer of energy and/or material between the two. If we apply this to organisations, then equlibrium can be reached by leadership keeping a steer on the framework and goal, whilst the employees have the freedom to fill out the framework in a way which meets the goal. Equilibrium is maintained whilst the two systems or functions contribute with what they are best at.

Build on nature's models and movement

The world of nature and physics engages many solutions from which a business can benefit. If you compare a microscopic picture of a pair of neutrons in the brain of a mouse with a simulated reproduction of what astrophysicists propose as the structure of the universe, with clusters of galaxies against dark matter, then the two images are almost identical. A mouse's neurons can be easily mistaken for a galactic system. When we study nature, we discover that its design is repeated in many variations at micro, meso, and macro scales. Many businesses have become interested in this, with the intention of copying nature's design and implementing the elements in their own systems. Over the past 3.8 billion years, nature has been in a process of trial and error to refine the living organisms, processes and materials which belong to Mother Earth. If the age of Earth was one calender year, then we humans developed 15 minutes ago and all written history would have happened in the past 60 seconds. We are being somewhat arrogant if we don't admit that it would be useful to us to imitate nature's design, when we need to find and create new forms of organisation for our businesses.

A robust characteristic of natural design is diversity. Nature is able to keep many variations open at the same time and this ability can be copied by businesses. If one variation of a natural system no longer functions, then nature can begin making use of other variations that function better under the new conditions. This form of evolution has been shown to occur as a leap to the next level, where new properties are suddenly seen to exist without the process taking several generations, which is what Darwin initially believed to be the case. Nature has the ability to *debrief* and as such to "know" what functions can best implement a change or set a movement free for the next level of development. In this way, nature's own design ensures its survival.

We can design businesses to do the same. One way to do this, is to work *with* nature, instead of believing that we are master *of* it. We are in nature and nature is in us. 70 percent of the earth is water. The same is true for the human body.

In agriculture, people are beginning to realise how important it is to maintain a diverse production of crops in order to avoid that disease hits the whole lot. One talks about copying nature's own regulatory mechanism. In the same way, most business leaders know that a system becomes vulnerable when it gets too rigid or too single minded. However, there are many businesses specialising more and more to get faster, and cheaper. This becomes like a huge form of agriculture with only one crop type. When the demand for this one crop falls, or suffers from disease, then the business immediately falls into crisis.

On our platform, and due to the movement that is set free when we decentralise power, responsibility, and decision-making, then we know not to specialise in details, but instead to be experts in synergetic processes between the units. Each unit can always develop new products which are adapted to their surrounding *biotope.*

It is not only in product development that one can incorporate nature's diversity, but also in the interplay between employees. The Danish service company, ISS implemented diversity by co-pying nature's design. They established their workforce using three criteria for diversity: first, they allowed a maximum of 70 percent men or women in any one area; second, they allowed a maximum of 70 percent to come from the same country, and third, they allowed a maximum of 70 percent to be of the same generation. This initiative increased ISS's profit by one and a half percent since sickleave in the more diverse teams decreased by 0.7 percent as compared to the non-diverse teams. This resulted in a net potential income of about 18 million US dollars per year. This increase cannot either be attributed to other factors such as differences in business areas, geography, team size, or seniority. It is primarily diversity that is the driver for the increased income so, it makes business sense to spend time creating a structure and team with diversity, just as nature does.

The knowledge and concepts we can develop on the basis of nature's design have become part of a discipline known as *biomimicry*. We can find great inspiration for solving man-made problems by looking at nature's models, systems, processes and elements. The word biomimicry comes from the greek, *bio*, meaning 'life', and *mimesis*, meaning 'to imitate'. Biomimicry is no new idea. As long as humans have been on earth, we have turned to nature in search of answers to simple and complex problems, and we have copied nature's patterns and production processes. Biomimicry is a prerequisite for creating new living systems and structures; again, platforms instead of silos.

Our current organisation design - hierarchical and separated in silos - assumes that some elements are more important than others and should therefore be given more power or influence. Instead, we need a design where all elements are equally important and can cooperate. This would lead to three structures:

1. The one that creates the frame or *context*.
2. The one that creates the *content*.
3. The one that ensures *cohesion* between context and content.

If we take Handelsbanken as an example, then top leadership created the context as a small handbook describing the goal, the means, and the philosophy. The content is produced by different departments, who organise themselves as they wish and choose the type of customer they want - citizen, farmer, or business. The regional directors are the facilitators who ensure cohesion between the handbook, as the context, and the departments, as the content.

This design imitates the design a proton has. A proton is made up of three quarks, two at the top and one at the bottom. The one at the bottom, the mediator, has the job of ensuring cohesion between the two others. It wouldn't make sense to ask which quark is most important. The three quarks make up a whole which cannot be split into anything smaller. In the same way, our organisations must be organisms which function as whole entities.

If we use the building blocks of the atom; protons, neutrons and electrons, can we then imagine an organisation diagram in which all three elements are present?

Let us look at which characteristics the three building blocks have in physics. Atoms consist of a core of protons and neutrons with electrons at the periphery. The proton represents the positive element (+), the neutron represents the neutral element (0), and the electron represents the negative element (-), or the balance. If we take nature's own design and use the qualities of the three elements in a business model, then we can create platforms that can understand the flexibility and motion that will be necessary in the future. The internationally renowned professor and biologist, Carsten Rahbek, of Copenhagen University, stated during House of Futures' 100-year project, that "we must learn to navigate the unknown."

The three structures with which I operate take their origin in the atom and can be expanded upon here, with reference to figure 13:

1. That which creates context (= framework), contributes with *flow*; that is, growth, freedom, and healthy competition. Context represents the positive element corresponding to the proton (+).
2. That which creates cohesion, contributes with *flex*; that is, flexibility, reciprocity, and collective spirit. Cohesion is represented by the neutron (0).
3. That which creates content, contributes with *form*; that is, sustainability, balance, and cooperation. The content grows from inside and out, and as such, creates substance as *form*. Content represents the negative element corresponding to the electron (-), which is a sign for balance.

If nature only had growth and not sustainability and cohesion, it wouldn't survive. A creeper plant, which grows so

Flow   Flex   Form

Context: Cohesion: Content:
Growth   Flexibility   Sustainability
Freedom   Reciprocity   Balance
Healthy competition Collective spirit   Cooperation

Proton (+)   Neutron (0)   Electron (-)

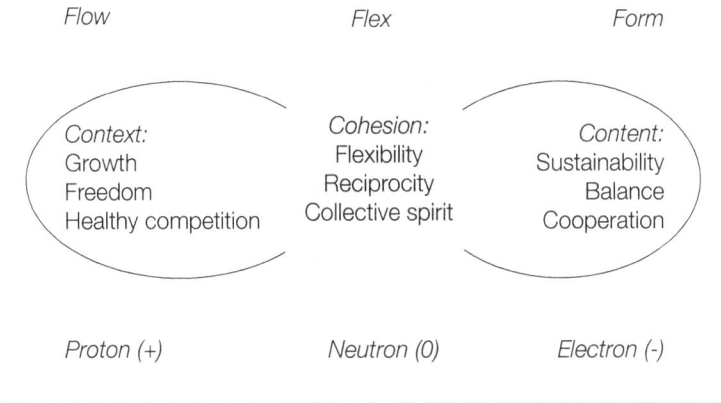

quickly that it hasn't managed to develop hooks to hold it up or offer resistance to winter weather, is not equipped to survive. In this case, the creeper has used all its energy on growth. This has the same effect as only growing one crop on all one's fields. Or, with the case of a cancer tumour, which grows and spreads on one path and eventually causes its own extinction.

We have discussed at length how the growth paradigm should be stopped and replaced by a new focus on sustainability. Norwegian Jørgen Randers and American *deep ecologist,* Donella Meadows, published *"The Limits to Growth"* in 1972. This was accompanied by a computer model showing the catastrophic consequences of an economic growth paradigm in a world of limited resources. When we consider things in the context of nature's models, it becomes clear that a one hundred percent focus on growth creates imbalance. We lack sustainability and cohesion. The same imbalance occurs, just to the opposite degree, with a one hundred percent focus on sustainability. In this case, we lack flow and flex. Companies without flow (growth) can be compared to water which can't flow; it sits still and becomes stagnant.

Biomimicry and nature's building blocks make it clear

that growth (flow), cohesion (flex) and sustainability (form) must be present in equal measures for a company to operate as a platform. Many business models contain elements of both competition and cooperation but lack cohesion, that is, the neutral element that enables things to work holistically rather than as fragmented departments; where, for example, the sales department works on growth, whilst other departments take care of production, HR, work-life balance, CSR and sustainability. Throughout the book, I have used different situations to introduce the three elements of flow, flex, and form. If we manage to use the design that is already present in nature and, in this case, use atomic structure as inspiration for our new organisation, we can make it a *blueprint* for the platform's building blocks.

Swarm theory

In his book *Ecological Intelligence,* Daniel Goleman writes: "Our brain is excellent at reacting to immediate threats, but is bad at dealing with the things that will threaten us in the future. Human perception has certain imperceptible boundaries or thresholds which block what occurs beneath," that is, things beyond what our senses can register. In other words, we don't possess sufficient senses for reading and reacting to things that happen or change slowly and subtly. Because of this, we continue with *business as usual.*

An organism, such as an ant colony, receives information from all individuals according to the swarm's *rules* or *plan.* The ant colony functions as a whole, in spite of it being made up of many different departments. According to the theory on swarms, which covers species such as fish, birds, bees, and ants, nature has preprogrammed a design that can both ensure growth and long-term sustainability. In his book, *Smart Swarm*, Peter Miller describes the advantages of operating like a swarm. Any one individual doesn't need to be smart for the swarm to be smart as a whole. This is possible due to the swarm's behaviour being coordinated via subtle information. For example, an ant colony has no leader and no hierarchy. The queen is no more important than the others. It is only us, humans that have placed her at the top of a hierarchy because this is the way our own system is organised. The queen's job is to lay eggs whilst other ants keep guard against dangers, bring in food or repair the anthill. All functions are essential for the survival and long-term sustainability of the ant colony.

A swarm is a self-organising system in which problem solving and control are decentralised. As a swarm, the ants are able to act collectively without each being told what to do. This allows them to create the ant colony as a holistic system that can serve the many. The employees of Morning Star work and achieve their common goal in exactly the same way. All ants in the ant colony rely on the local information they receive. This local information works in the same way as the overriding goal or context of the self-organising system. A change in the context requires that the new information issued, is strong enough to create a new pattern or provide new meaning to the swarm. If the context changes, then the entire system changes. This is precisely what makes the swarm sustainable, since it allows the present swarm to develop in a way best for them without limiting the chances for future generations to meet their needs. This is possible because changes are allowed to occur gradually without the swarm being forced to act against its will by one individual. It is only by a sufficiently large number of individuals seeing the same pattern, that change can occur. This moment of change is known as a *tipping point*. The key to survival is the mediation between the needs of the swarm and the needs of the individual. The result is more than the sum of the single individuals' demands. A self-organising system such as a swarm is decentralised. Problem solving is distributed and delegated.

Continuous interaction among individuals creates more value for all. To be able to meet present needs without compromising those of future generations is precisely the definition of sustainability as proposed in the UN report, the Brundtland Report, *"Our Common Future"* from 1987.

Swarms favour improvements to the system by choosing a particular pattern created via interaction between the many individuals. There is a high degree of knowledge sharing and awareness in terms of which role one is playing in serving the whole. The behaviour that a company can copy from a swarm is:

- to favour improvements (flow/context)
- to share what you learn (flex/facilitator)
- to understand how you influence (form/content)

The element, flex, makes it possible for change and adjustments to occur between flow and form when local information changes and as long as everyone keeps sharing what they learn. The three elements; flow, flex and form are the basis of a prototype for a platform organisation.

In Novo Nordisk, the context changed when the *Novo Nordisk Way* was introduced. Novo's facilitators received ongoing updates from each employee if something wasn't working in the existing context. This information was then passed on to the leadership who could then change the overriding context.

A movement is an ongoing relation

James P. Carse, Professor in Religion at New York University, presents in his book, *Finite and Infinite Games*, a theory that there are two kinds of games: complete and incomplete. In a complete game, one plays to win. In an incomplete game one plays to keep the game going. If the game rules mean that the game is about to end, or that a player is about to lose, then the rules must be changed such that the game can continue with equal advantage to all players. Everyone is a winner in an incomplete game because most important are process, inclusion and holism. When caucasian Australians were teaching the Aborigines to play football, the native inhabitants didn't understand the concept of the sport. They just kept on playing until both teams had an equal number of goals. Aborigines feel that it isn't fun to spend the rest of the day with someone who has lost. Making sure that everyone feels comfortable and included in the group is more important than building up a hierarchy in which an individual's performance is credited at the cost of the group. Aborigines didn't understand football because it's a win-lose sport.

Carse has proposed a series of preconditions for complete and continuous (incomplete) games which are important for a company to know if they want to maintain an ongoing movement and survive long-term:

– The rules of a complete game cannot be changed.
– The rules of a continuous game change in order to avoid anyone winning the game and to include as many people in the game as possible.
– The language used in a continuous game is alive and *in process*, for example "agree" or "don't agree", whilst words like "right" or "wrong" belong to the complete game.
– Complete games are serious since one fights to win whilst continuous games are entertaining since it is the process and the learning involved that are most important.
– A player in a complete game consumes time, whilst a player in a incomplete game generates time since, in the latter case, time is used to nurture ongoing relationships and existence.
– Complete games can be played as continuous games as long as the players don't interpret their roles as finished, and can continue to develop under new relationships.

When a company is in movement, it is able to change the context or overriding goal if the game is about to end. Once Jan Carlzon as CEO for SAS had reached the goal that was set for his company, both leadership and employees lost their energy. The game was over and everyone was victorious. Carlzon then looked for a new vision for SAS which the employees could be just as passionate about. But such a goal takes time to establish. Before it was discovered and accepted, the company found itself in a vacuum. The former leader of Danish trade union committee, *LO*, Thomas Nielsen, had the same experience as Jan Carlzon when he expressed these famous words about the unions: "We have won right to hell." If an organisation or company cannot change its context, or goal, then there is no movement and flow towards an end.

If you keep doing the same thing as you've always done, in the same way, then at one point you will start to run yourself down, since the rest of the world is constantly changing. What used to work, doesn't work anymore. A goal or context must therefore be changed to suit.

The movement's success

When a company is in movement and has created a platform for cooperation between the individual departments, a dynamic is created which corresponds to the one we know from, for example, Wikipedia. This open source encyclopedia, which is created by and for the users, functions in accordance with the principles behind swarm theory: favour improvements; share what you learn; and understand how you influence.

Wikipedia has put together a platform, with a flexible structure, which uses its resources to find, connect, and support those users who share the same aim. Wikipedia was launched with the aim of providing underprivileged children access to a good encyclopedia. Today, Wikipedia contains more than 24 million accessible articles in 285 languages, written by over 36 million registered users and has countless anonymous contributors all over the world. It is the world's sixth most popular website and it is used every month by nearly 13 percent of all internet users. According to an analysis published in *Psychological Medicine*, Wikipedia's information is more accurate than classical literature.

The story of Wikipedia speaks for itself in terms of what a movement can achieve. It shows us how vital it is to be able to create cooperative and continuous games; games in which everyone wants to contribute, as long as the purpose and vision are attractive enough. Wikipedia has voluntary

> **"The most important thing you can do to achieve your goals is to make sure that as soon as you set them, you immediately begin to create momentum".**
>
> *– Anthony Robbins*

control-users or facilitators who ensure cohesion between the platform's context and those who provide free knowledge. If anyone uploads incorrect or offensive material to the website, then they can remove or edit it.

A company that wants to create a platform must, like Wikipedia, hold on to its context, but be open and empathetic towards its employees and contributors, by giving them the freedom, responsibility and space to find their own way to serve the common purpose.

Holistic responsibility and maturity are preconditions

An organisation is no more or better than the people in it. When a company creates a formal structure, the organisation is not truly functioning, until its people know and fulfill their own role in the structure. Whether a company is ready to set the platform in motion and possesses the maturity it needs, is determined by two factors. Firstly, do the leaders and employees have the personal ability to make their own aim to work well with others and contribute in making content for the structure? Secondly, do the leaders and employees know their function with respect to the bigger structure and fulfill it in relation to the entire organisation?

Maturity is present on the platform when leaders and employees possess the three qualities of flow, form, and flex and make full use of this potential in and for the company. We are still novices in the art of cooperation. Our human species is young, but we must learn how to work together, and sooner rather than later. One person is perhaps good at creating the context, and articulating the overriding goal (flow). Another is maybe good at implementing new initiatives and getting things done (form). A third is perhaps best at getting people to work together, creating team spirit and maintaining positive relationships (flex). When we contribute with what we are best at, together with others who do the same, then we mature.

The immature elements in a business will, for example, obstruct knowledge-sharing, limit the space for improvement or refuse to take responsibility for the way they influence the company. The company won't be able to function as a swarm, and the platform will be denied any form of movement. To afford the many advantages that exist in the movement requires a high level of consciousness, responsibility, and integrity.

Søren Ulslev was CEO for the Danish building contractor, NCC, and is currently CEO for the Danish building contractor, MT Højgaard. He helped set up a *"partnering"* concept at NCC, which was designed to increase business potential by forming mutually beneficial relationships with customers and other companies. In the process, it became clear that not all employees were open or tolerant enough to support this initiative. To prevent delay or further obstacles, NCC had to let these employees go. When customers approached NCC in order to initiate a partnering agreement, Søren Ulslev would always check their background, beliefs, and values. If these didn't match the aims and context for "partnering" - including mutual trust, openness, and responsibility - then this form of collaboration wouldn't be possible.

As described earlier, it is our beliefs that drive our work. Therefore, it is essential that all employees are both conscious of, and in agreement with, the beliefs that support operations on the platform. In the animal kingdom, relationships and cohesion are basic and natural properties for ensuring survival. In his book, Dyret i dit spejl (*The Animal in Your Mirror),* Bent Jørgensen describes how a vampire bat won't share the blood it sources from other animals with just any member of its own flock. Research shows that it will first and foremost share with other bats who have been similarly generous towards them. This means that these bats keep a record of reciprocity within the course of their relationships. In a business, this task will fall to the facilitator. They will facilitate anyone who doesn't operate according to the premises of the platform, and eventually dismiss anyone who keeps failing to do so. The company needs to hold tight to its framework (context) in order to keep the platform together, but still show empathy towards all its stakeholders in order to support and help them in the process.

The movement's turning point

In recent years, a lot has been written about critical mass; that is, the number of people it takes to activate a certain situation or movement. How many people need to support a leader in order for a system to accept a new idea? In silos, companies can introduce new procedures by the leadership giving orders or devising new rules for the employees to follow. On the platform, a company can bring in something new by creating a *"following"*. This involves employees following their leader along a new path, voluntarily and because they want to.

In his book, *The Tipping Point: How Little Things Can Make a Big Difference*, author and journalist, Malcolm Gladwell describes how, in every system, there is a time when things begin to move in a new direction. The turning point is the critical point in every situation or relationship that leads to a new or changed condition, and that cannot be changed back to the way things were before. Gladwell believes the lack of consciousness around this point means that some leaders stop the evolution of a positive change just before turning point is reached. In doing so, they fall short of the change they had hoped for, and which was just about to happen had they let the process continue a while longer. The leadership gives up, convincing themselves that it wasn't working anyway. Many good intentions and actions are lost on this altar because there hasn't been sufficient knowledge that a turning point exists. Michael Møllmann from Novo Nordisk says: "One shouldn't turn back when in the middle of crossing a river." (see his interview on page 173).

When you, as the leader of a company, begin a new movement, it is comparable to pushing a car into motion after its motor has stopped. In the beginning, it is hard to shift it, but once rolling, less force is needed to keep it moving. One sharp and deliberate push can set the movement going. Once we gain more speed and momentum, this attracts people who want to be part of the movement. The case of Wikipedia is a good example to illustrate this.

Besides momentum, it is important to create critical mass in order for the movement to grow. Recent research has shown that there is a key number or level at which a turning point is likely to occur. This discovery was published in the article, "*Social consensus through the influence of committed minorities*". Researchers at the Rensselaer Polytechnic Institute, USA, found that when ten percent of a population share the same indisputable opinion or belief, their opinion will be accepted by a majority of the population. This result has great impact on companies and social interaction; affecting how innovation can spread and how political ideals can be altered. Ten percent is the critical mass required to set a movement going and implement a company's new platform. As stated by one of the group's researchers: "When the number of engaged opinion makers is under ten percent, then there is no visible progress of ideas." The researchers analyzed the growth of opinion using computer models and different social networks. Regardless of the type of network being studied, ten percent remained the turning point for changing the opinion of the majority.

In order to create a movement on the platform, you, as leader, must gain the support and following of atleast ten percent of the company's strongest opinion makers. As organisation entrepreneur, Derek Sivers says in his TED talk on how to start a movement: "The first follower is what transforms a lone nut into a leader."

The movement – *Summary*

A flexible structure uses its resources to find, connect, and support those who share the same objective for achieving a specific result. When there is movement on the platform, then the traditional system is turned on its head as employees and leaders are equally important. The following points are key characteristics for a movement:

– It uses the system's inner *flow*, energy and resources to reach its goal.
– Its structure resembles nature's design for protons, electrons, and neutrons.
– It operates as a swarm and, as such, functions as a community.
– If the game begins to reach its end, the structure or context changes in order to form a series of continuous and lasting relationships.
– It is dependent on the awareness and responsibility of all employees and leaders.
– It is only set in motion if a minumum of ten percent of the employees support the cause.

INTRO

The interview with Michael Møllmann, corporate vice-president at Novo Nordisk A/S,
shows what happens when the three elements of *servant leadership*, *personal leadership* and *facilitation* are united. You can
read how Michael Møllmann used all three
elements in the organisation and what the
reactions were.

Belief moves mountains

From the outside, the Device Manufacturing & Sourcing plant looks like any other streamline factory building. However, as soon as one steps inside, it buzzes with life. We are here at Novo Nordisk A/S, Hillerød, to meet corporate vice-president, Michael Møllmann. Michael is the head of 400 employees who are responsible for the plastic components for all Novo's different products. This business area works with almost a thousand people from different manufacturers and suppliers across the world. They have doubled their production in just four years without any change to the workforce. Over the same period, accidents in the work place dropped from ten to zero, and sick leave has decreased from five to three percent per year. We discussed with Michael what he's done and does as a leader to bring about such changes.

What is good leadership for you?
"It always begins and ends with people. The rest is just about tools. It's about faith and not only behaviour, competence or structure. It's about leadership principles, the creation of culture and the way we relate to others. My focus is that everyone contributes to the creation of value. I believe that everyone can take decisions and that together we can create a place where everyone is happy. If you create good platforms for people then they want to stay and give their all. We don't use a lot of resources on replacing employees, since they usually want to stay."

How have you gained this insight?
"I have a background as a civil engineer with an MBA and an HD. I have an operational education, specialising in mathematical modelling. Early on in my career within production management, I recognised that I could only use my technical skills to understand the ins and outs of production. I could see that it was only by working with other people that I could accomplish bigger things and fulfill my dreams. Everyday, I focus on offering a better life to the patients who are dependent upon our products, whilst at the same time making sure that each of my 400 employees are happy in their work. This is a huge challenge in a world undergoing such great changes. Today, change is part of life. While all our employees have accepted this, they are still against much of what change brings."

How does change affect you as a leader?
"There is never a moment of calm. In time gone, a business leader could sit behind his mahogany desk far from the production floor and use reports and middle management to stay in charge. Today, it is essential that company leaders are present at the place where value is created. This is why I don't have an office, only a shoulder bag. I am forced to stay on the move, and be present where things happen."

The transformation
How was the organisation when you took over?
"When I took over the organisation four years ago, I could see that there were some rigid silos which had been put up and which needed to be brought down."

Why do you think these silos were created?
"This was an area which had achieved good results because those leading it had focussed on being the best in their own individual departments. There were clear, well-defined areas of work and a high degree of internal competition. This can be an extremely strong way to run a business as long as one can maintain an overview whilst each employee focusses

only on what happens within their own box. You get a great deal of production output like this, but not much human output, and no employee wants to stay in the same job for very long because the culture is so hard. Each employee has their own field of work, and they are expected to stick to it. When I came here four years ago there were employees at one end of the building pointing fingers at those at the other end. It was as if they were saying, "we reached our targets, and you didn't reach yours!"

What did you do to bring the silos down?
"We implemented two things within the first seven weeks: A new vision, and an organisational change initiative that removed all the silos. We created a vision that everyone could relate to. I sat down with each leader to establish their individual competences. One of these leaders had developed a vision for their own department, illustrated by climbing the mountain of BiC (Best in Class). We chose this image for the entire business area since one can apply BiC to everything; production, support, quality assurance etc. The beauty of BiC is that one is never done with it. It is a continual search for excellence. The leader mentioned was given free rein to implement the vision process for all the other leaders. We built a three metre high BiC mountain out of polystyrene for use in a vision-seminar where everyone was present (see page 213). At the beginning of this seminar I was asked what BiC meant for me and what the top of the mountain looked like. Everyone stood round thinking that they could each climb their particular side of the mountain without much difficulty. Therefore, they were much surprised by my vision for the entire workforce to climb the mountain together without splitting off into separate silos. This brought people out of the silos because people wanted to succeed with their teams. This required cooperation. As in any mountaineering expedition, everyone involved needed to climb at the same time, reach the camp positions together, and help anyone falling behind.

A four year vision was created. We knew which culture we wanted, which goals we were striving for, and which methods to use. I left the seminar in the morning of the second day and when I returned later the same day, the mountain was finished. This was the result of an *aligned* movement, in which every layer of the organisation had moved in the three-dimensional reality of the BiC mountain, rather than the two-dimensions described by a typical organisations diagram or image. There has been slight adjustments along the way, but we have already achieved 80 to 90 percent of what we set out to achieve. Now, we have reached so high that we are able to see other mountain summits. So there will soon be another mountain which we need to create and climb together.

Trust in the expedition leader and passion for the project

It sounds simple, but what is the most important element in such a process?
"Two things. First, that people believe in the leader, and second, that people believe in the project. They need to want to be part of the journey and have trust in whoever is to take the lead. It is about trust and belief. As such, after one year, we found two sisters for the BiC principles: trust and belief. Trust is seen and felt in the faith, care and love that we show towards one another. Trust is the basis for delegation. I don't control those I delegate to. Many of my colleagues don't understand why it is hard for them to delegate. As I see it, they are too busy trying to seize control, which is often explained by the widespread focus on evaluation and reviews. But you can get people to fly to the moon if they have the desire and passion to get there."

Do you think that trust is something we are born with, or something we can learn?
"It can definitely be learned. Personally, I trust before I mistrust. It is vital that we talk about trust in the course of our

everyday life, for example, by discussing what is good behaviour and what is not. When we have chosen trust as a leadership principle, then we need to articulate this each and everyday."

What does job-title or salary mean in this context?
"When salary is below a certain level then it means everything. When, on the other hand, salary exceeds this level, then it starts to carry very little meaning. I make a distinction between what you feel like doing, and what you need to do. Salary has no real meaning as long as people receive the payment that matches their expectations. What matters is that people trust in their leader and the project since this is what motivates them to run the extra mile. Silos are pulled down and a collective spirit is created when everyone moves in the same direction towards the same goal. In our field, job-titles mean nothing internally but everything in terms of our external relations when we work with European, American, Chinese or Brazilian partners."

Servant leaders create good employees

In leadership circles, you have been called a "servant leader".
Can you tell us about this?
At the start, I wasn't aware that the way I lead is called "servant leadership". That became clear to me about five years ago. My journey towards servant leadership began with the conviction that being a good leader meant being a good companion. I am an active, critical and constructive companion myself and I always strive to support my boss the best I can. This too is the type of companion that I look for. In order to make my leaders into the best companions then I need to make them good at doing what they do each day. As such, I have become the kind of leader who believes that when I make my employees good, then I too am good. It begins with them and it demands that I really understand their needs. It is their needs I should serve and not their desires.

Once I establish their needs, I can then support them on the journey towards our common goal.

When I read Robert Greenleafs book, "Servant Leadership", in which he names Jesus as the first servant leader, it first occurred to me how Jesus had served his disciples in order for them to serve him. I have tried to do the same – without further comparison to this particular figure of course!"

How do you tackle your ego?
"This is a good question. Actually, I haven't given this much thought, so perhaps this doesn't mean too much to me in day to day life. If I make my leaders good, then I'm good. It's this way around, not the opposite. It is much more important to me how the organisation can be *Best in Class,* and what's more, this is much more exciting. My quest is to create the best organisation for the leader who someday will replace me. I can do this by building a structure and a culture to make the employees want to take responsibility. Today, the organisation can run for long periods at a time without me needing to get involved. My job is to think strategically and long-term. I delegate to the best leaders according to the strategic framework we have created together.

How come there aren't more people doing the same as you?
"In my experience this comes down to fear. People are afraid of changing *themselves,* but if change is to happen, this is the only place to start. The way I lead is very different from the way my colleagues lead. Often, one has been promoted from middle management to top leadership by being good at a particular type of leadership. But staying successful in a position of leadership today requires that one embraces a new motive and new methods, and this takes courage. One needs to stop controlling and start delegating responsibility instead. One needs to offer much more of oneself. One needs to get out of one's own office and the meeting room and get close to where value is created. As the kind of leader I am, I

Novo Nordisk Way – 10 Essentials is a list of statements to describe how Novo Nordisk works in practice. The 10 Essentials are designed to help leaders and employees measure how well their business area is performing in relation to the Novo Nordisk Way. As such, the 10 Essentials are a useful tool in highlighting any gaps to be filled or areas to be improved in order to get even closer to the values inherent within Novo Nordisk:

1. We create value by having a patient centred business approach
2. We set ambitious goals and strive for excellence.
3. We are accountable for our financial, environmental and social performance.
4. We provide innovation to the benefit of our stakeholders.
5. We build and maintain good relations with our key stakeholders.
6. We treat everyone with respect.
7. We focus on personal performance and development.
8. We have a healthy and engaging working environment.
9. We optimise the way we work and strive for simplicity.
10. We never compromise on quality and business ethics.

---

need everyone to take responsibility for the whole and not least for themselves. In this way, employees must also become servant leaders for the whole. They must believe in their quest. As a leader, it is crucial to keep one's finger on the pulse of any actual or potential process of change. For this reason, I meet with all leaders in our area for one afternoon each month. In the beginning, we called this *Change Tracking*, but now we call it the *Leadership Timeout*! At these meetings, we discuss our difficult cases and the changes we have been through. We develop our leadership principles and act as *coach* for one another. These meetings are critical for me to keep track of any change in culture. It isn't an easy journey, so it is vital that I know precisely where we are and where we are heading. I cannot waver along the way. When others from the leadership come by, they don't understand how we have embarked on so much at once or how much we have accomplished in such a short time. The explanation is that our method of delegating responsibility is working. There are far fewer bottle-necks to obstruct development, and not one leader preventing us from moving forward. It comes down to keeping our focus on the whole and on the direction; on the *flow*. Its all about speed and wholeness."

Why do some people not understand?
"If you look at our organisation and structure without explanation, then it looks simple enough on the surface. But what lies deeper and between the lines can't be seen. I've watched how some of my colleagues, in the hope of following suit, copy our structure and grab the tools without first having understood our underlying culture and the motivation which drives us. Implementing an entirely new culture demands a conscious decision and complete belief in the idea. Once you embark on crossing the stream it can get very deep on the way and it will take at least a year, if not two, to get to the other side. It isn't enough for the leaders to just listen, they must believe. What is key, is the recognition that, in any organisation, people want to develop and they want their freedom."

Leader as facilitator
How do you facilitate your three leadership principles; trust, passion and BiC via NOVO Nordic Way?
The facilitators at NOVO Nordic A/S think that what we are doing is fantastic. Our culture is both challenging and comfortable and this allows everyone to believe in the leadership principles behind NOVO Nordic Way. We must lead with trust in our employees and have confidence in our facilitators to hold us to the value base of the company. If you don't comply to NOVO Nordic Way, then you are not allowed passed the gate. In this case, you will be subject to an audit with instructions for what needs to change. If, on the other hand, you already follow NOVO Nordic Way, then your be-

haviour will be used as an example of best practice for other business areas. In this way, the facilitators at NOVO Nordic A/S act as the link between the different areas of the company. I myself, have worked as a facilitator part-time, in order to better understand this function. I follow my section leaders like a shadow. I act as their facilitator, asking the right questions, listening, observing staying up to date with their activities. I spend one or two mornings each month with each leader helping them to develop and become better at what they do. To be true to my own mission and to be better at my job, I need to work with these leaders continuously and keep giving them my feedback. The intention is to instill a better flow to their everyday life. The leaders at Novo don't have a quiet life. They are constantly challenged. As an analogy, you should feel as though you're on a heated seat on a hot summer's day; that is, uncomfortable but ok."

Building cathedrals, not just chiselling bricks

Do you believe that Danish culture has a competitive advantage on the international market?

"We have a strong position to start with here since analysis has rated the Danes as being amongst the most trustworthy people in the world. This allows us to create organisations where trust is paramount. But, we need to want to do this. We need to seek trust and cultivate it. If we only use commands and control and construct silos, then we won't yield the fruits of this trust. The potential exists, but we need to use it actively. The environment in a silo corresponds to the bottom layer of Gary Hamel's pyramid, in which employees obey orders, but only carry out the tasks that their title describes (see page 182). You need to make yourself worthy of receiving people's passion, creativity and initiative. Employees need to have trust in both you and the project. They need to contribute to building the cathedral and not only chisel the bricks. We Danes can build cathedrals well but it is also possible that we won't. The potential is here and I can feel that it's been set free in my company. Our structure has

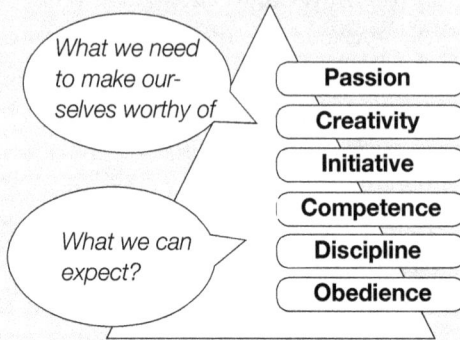

become a platform built on trust and companionship. Unfortunately, many modern leadership methods are based on mistrust. One often sets KPI's based on mistrust. Even small issues can be passed through five levels of management before anyone acts. Our system generates resources, trust, a positive mindset and profit on the bottom line.

Can everyone work in this way?
"I haven't yet met an employee that can't, despite the fact that many are cautious when facing something new. In general, the problem is not the employees but the leaders, since they often have great difficulty in relinquishing their control. I believe that in many companies, we have harboured a mass of control freaks. We have forgotten to give our leaders the right tools and structures to lead in a new way."

What are you looking for when you employ new leaders to your organisation?
"Leaders with high self-esteem. They must feel content with themselves and not open the conversation with the results they have achieved, but rather by talking about the people they have worked with. When I spoke about trust and companionship at the beginning of our change process, then these may have well been cities on the moon as far as some

of our leaders were concerned. Today, these same people have moved themselves to another place entirely. They have managed to open a series of extra channels. For some, these channels get blocked easily which means that they must constantly be told what to do. I would have great difficulty having this kind of leader in our organisation."

How can leaders learn to trust?
"One can learn *about* trust by reading, but one cannot learn to trust by reading alone. The most important is to practise. I have read many interesting books about servant leadership and strength-based leadership but there are three instances that really opened my eyes. It is no secret that I started out as a control freak. Very quickly, I was thrown so many direct questions and handed so many problems that I didn't have time to control all of them. In certain periods, I had to let go of this control, and to my surprise things started to get better! Despite me feeling anxious about letting go, this triggered a form of deep reflection. The second instance was when I heard a lecture on spiritual intelligence. I learned that belief is one of the strongest motivational forces that exist. Fundamentally, belief is driven by trust and companionship to and between people. This made me curious to discover how much one could achieve in a position of leadership by creating a dream that everyone could believe in. The third instance was when I saw the power of giving employees responsibility at work and encouraging them to take responsibility for their own lives. Before this point, I had become completely drained of energy when conducting personal development appraisals with my staff since I was so busy trying to direct the conversation. I remember thinking that if I continued like this I would simply have to quit being a leader. But then it occurred to me that it wasn't about me, but about *them*. It was the employees who should speak for themselves and voice their own ideas. I shouldn't use so much of my own energy but rather draw out *their* needs and ask about *their* development. It isn't my place to

suggest a template for how others should be. In this way, I shouldn't take responsibility away from them, but trust that they can take it for themselves."

A network for the like-minded

What are your dreams for the future?
"The wild dream is that even more people at NOVO Nordic A/S or other companies start to work in this way. I'd like to meet them and cooperate with them, since it is sometimes a lonely quest. I would like to be part of a network of like-minds. One meets suprisingly few business leaders who are following this route. This is a shame, because it's good for people in terms of acting against stress *and* it improves your company's bottom line. It saddens me that so much goes to waste. I want to prove how this way of working produces happiness as well as results. Some years ago, I interviewed one of the top chief executives at NOVO Nordic as part of my MBA. He told me that he wasn't sure how possible it was to create a really cooperative team at the level of top leadership because too many people at this level have too big an ego. They tend to want to prove that others are wrong. Therefore the first step I made was to form a top leadership team in which we make each other good by trusting and supporting one another. There is enough work for everyone and we don't need to stand in each other's way."

THE WORLD AS IT SHOULD BE

"The decadent international but individualistic capitalism, in the hands of which we found ourselves after the war, is not a success. It is not intelligent, it is not beautiful, it is not just, it is not virtuous – and it doesn't deliver the goods. In short we dislike it, and we are beginning to despise it. But when we wonder what to put in its place, we are extremely perplexed!"

– Economist, John Maynard Keynes,
The Yale Review, june 1933

"Hope is not blind optimism. It's not ignoring the enormity of the task ahead or the roadblocks that stand in our path. It's not sitting on the sidelines or shirking from a fight. Hope is that thing inside us that insists, despite all evidence to the contrary, that something better awaits us if we have the courage to reach for it, and to fight for it. Hope is the belief that destiny will not be written for us, but by us, by the men and women who are not content to settle for the world as it is, who have the courage to remake the world as it should be."

– Barack Obama, presidential address,
6th November 2012

CHAPTER 9

The Butterfly Effect

This chapter is about what happens when we combine the platform's three elements of flow, flex, and form. You will begin to gain an understanding for how these three qualities support each other and can lead to a dynamic company which is able to both serve itself and its surrounding context. You will be introduced to the role each element plays in the company in terms of *servant leadership*, *facilitation* and *personal leadership*. You will be given the recipe for a company model which I call *The Butterfly Effect*, and which is intelligent, beautiful, and fair.

A new company model
The formula for a new platform's company model consists of three key elements: flow, flex, and form. These three elements or qualities are made operational when translated into three functions for a new company model, The Butterfly. The three functions are as follows:

- Servant Leadership is responsible for growth and *flow* and for creating the platform's context as a resource and as an opportunity to contribute to a common and over-riding goal.
- The facilitator is responsible for cohesion or *flex*. Their role is to facilitate others and ensure that all content lies within its context and that the context, in turn, supports its content.
- Personal leadership is responsible for sustainability or *form*, such that the employees can contribute content via input of labour, wisdom, and cooperation.

"Never doubt that a small group of thoughtful, committed citizens can change the world. Indeed it is the only thing that ever has."

– Margaret Mead, Anthropologist

Fig. 14 on the opposite page shows what the three functions look like when they are configured to work together as a whole. The structure that is created contains both order and chaos and can accommodate this tension with the help of a facilitator. The image of chaotic flow is shown by using the Lorenz attractor and takes the form of a butterfly (see page 151). As such, the new company model is named, *The Butterfly Effect*.

Before I move into the advantages of this three-fold system, I will introduce each element in the following order; servant leadership, personal leadership and the role of the facilitator. Each element and its characteristics have the potential to transform silos into platforms.

Servant leadership – creating the context

The term *"servant leadership"* was coined in 1970 by Robert Greenleaf to describe the approach employed by a leader whose primary aim is to serve the collective and its particular needs. Such a leader first defines themselves as a leader when they have a vision that can serve the collective.

Greenleaf worked as a developer for one of the world's largest tele-providers AT&T, but chose early retirement in order to set up the *Center for Applied Ethics* in 1964 as an alternative organisation to the one governed by command and control leadership. He was affiliated to large universities such as MIT and Harvard Business School as a teacher and inspirator. When management guru and professor, Peter Senge delivered a speech in 1992 at the Greenleaf Centre's annual conference, and subsequently published his *"Reflec-*

FIGURE 14: THE BUTTERFLY EFFECT

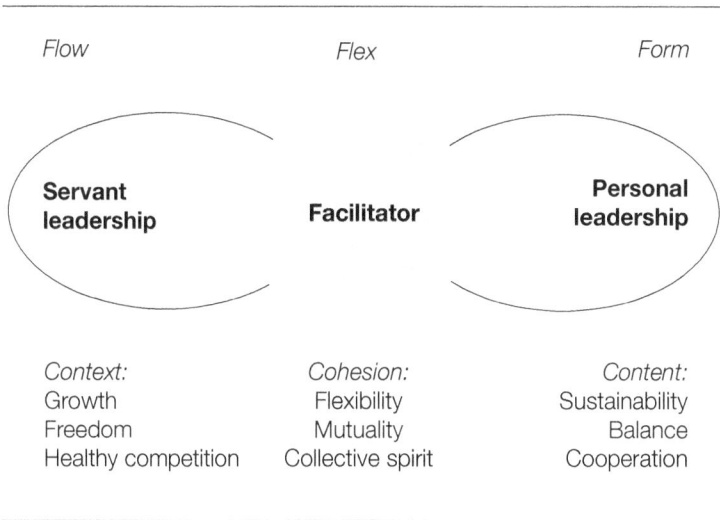

Flow   *Flex*   *Form*

Servant leadership	**Facilitator**	**Personal leadership**

Context:	*Cohesion:*	*Content:*
Growth	Flexibility	Sustainability
Freedom	Mutuality	Balance
Healthy competition	Collective spirit	Cooperation

tions on Leadership", he remarked, "The book, *Servant Leadership,* and in particular the initial chapter about the servant as leader, is one of the most unique and relevant statements on leadership which I have read in the past twenty years."

Servant leadership makes it possible for both leadership and the company as a whole to serve a higher purpose and set its employees free. Servant leadership is about having power *with* the employees rather than over them. Figure 15 (see next page) compares a silo's command and control leadership with a model for servant leadership. A key characteristic of servant leadership is that the leader is genuinely engaged in functioning as a beacon, showing how it is possible to both serve oneself and one's environment. There is a direct relationship between the quality of a community or environment and how likely it is for a business in this environment to succeed. It is important that such leadership characteristics are allowed to come into play.

Greenleaf refers to the Danish theologian and author, N.F.S. Grundtvig, as a person with servant leadership char-

	Command and control	Servant leadership
Image / perception of the company	The organisation is a static machine	The organisation is structured as an organism via relationships
Leadership	Top-down - centralised	Synergetic - decentralised
Employees	Instruments to produce	Greatest asset and source of innovation
Leadership style	Distant. Uses budgets	Connected and personal
Supervisor's Behaviour	Dictates, Controls, Punishes	Listens, encourages, motivates
Service approach	Serves itself: What can you do for me, What can you do for the company?	Serves others: What can I do to help you fulfil your superordinate goal?

acteristics. Grundtvig had a vision for how former tenants could learn to take on responsibility for themselves, once controls were lifted and they were given the option to own land.

This required that the tenants renewed their self-confidence and sought to gain new knowledge.

To help meet these needs, Grundtvig founded the public *højskole* (high school for over 16-year-olds) as a place for farmers to meet and support one another. As servant leader, Grundtvig carried the vision, but depended upon Christen Kold and Peter Hiort Lorenzen as facilitators to ensure that the high schools became a reality, and that yet more farmers learnt to take responsibility for themselves and adopt personal leadership in their own lives *(read more on Grundtvig in the interview with researcher, Sune Auken on page 205).*

Robert Greenleaf describes how a leader is first and foremost a servant – and not first and foremost a leader. The dif-

> **"I have not the shadow of a doubt that any man or woman can achieve what I have, if he or she would make the same effort and cultivate the same hope and faith."**
>
> – *Mahatma Gandhi*

ference lies in the fact that the servant leader makes it their business to fulfill other people's needs. The test for this kind of leader is to check whether the employees are developing holistically as people, whether they are becoming healthier, wiser, more free, more autonomous, and as a result, more adept at serving others. Serving others should not be misunderstood as putting oneself in an inferior position or creating any form of hiearchy.

To serve someone or something, is derived from a wish to give, simply *wanting* to, and not because one expects anything in return. The relationship between a servant leader and the employees is under constant development because as the employees grow, so too does the leader, and in turn, so does the company. As Michael Møllmann from NOVO Nordic A/S says: "When I make my employees good, I too become good" (read his interview on page 173) . Whenever it isn't working, a facilitator can step in to recreate the balance between the two functions of servant leadership and personal leadership.

Servant leadership is a more developed and mature form for leadership than the kind of traditional leadership we know today. It isn't about scoring the largest salary or highest bonus. The platform's leaders are driven by different factors, namely a desire to serve a larger collective than themselves. It is here they gain satisfaction, motivation, and reward.

It is vital for the platform that the company's management adopts the role of a servant leadership. It is of equal importance that the employees are ready and sufficiently mature to adopt personal leadership. Implicit to servant leadership is the belief that the company can achieve the best results when the best person for the task is allowed to steer. Such an organisation will therefore see different people taking a leadership position, with particular strengths in either defining the context or filling out its content. When the vision drawn up by a servant leader has been accomplished, they will be replaced by another, unless of course the same leader can create a second vision which is equally as captivating and which has just as much meaning as the first.

The employees in an organisation stay whilst the direction of flow or vision can change. Jan Carlzon from SAS is an example of a servant leader who chose to continue even though, as he admits himself, he should probably have considered leaving SAS once his vision was complete (see his interview on page 25),

Servant leadership strives to anticipate the future and lead a group of employees towards their goal by keeping the focus on *their* interests and continuously supporting them to be better. This creates a form of *fellowship* in which the employees want to follow their leader because they can see how he or she is acting in their interests. This happens from inside the organisation and from the bottom up rather than being pushed down from the above as in a typical hierarchical structure. Therefore, the first follower is even more important than the leader because the leader's is only here on behalf of the employees.

Frodo, the hobbit from Tolkien's *The Lord Of The Rings*, would prefer to stay home in the Shire than venture out on a mission to save mankind, elf folk and dwarves, in a fight against evil. Frodo is another example of a character who adopts servant leadership. Frodo is chosen as leader of a group of the greatest, strongest and wisest heroes because of his qualities of humility, honesty, authenticity, and compassion. Frodo is the only one whom everyone trusts to serve the whole group and the whole purpose of the quest. These qualities are the essence of servant leadership and there lies

"Take responsibility for instead of taking control of"

Who am I?	Identity	Real commitment to lead, create context for development and serve needs holistically, for a sustainable world
Why is what I do important, and which beliefs drive me?	Values	Non-exploitative authentic, compassionate and non-judgemental
What is my potential / competences	Competences	Knowledge of mental models systemic thinking, team learning, vision building
How do I behave?	Behaviour	Recognise, motivate and create self-worth
Which context do I create?	Environment	Respect for the whole and development potential

a Frodo in you that can be awakened, since all of us can bring these qualities forth if we really want to.

Servant Leadership gives us associations of characters such as Frodo, Gandhi, Martin Luther King, Kennedy and Mother Teresa, but the characteristics necessary for practising servant leadership are not only limited to the few. As Michael Møllmann from NOVO Nordic A/S tells us in his interview (see page 173), he himself wasn't aware that he was employing servant leadership although this was precisely what he was doing.

Another great inspiration is the manual written by Dee Hock for VISA International. Hock describes how, after many years of leadership in a large international company, he practised servant leadership: "Make a careful list of all

Associates: Hire and promote first on the basis of integrity; second, motivation; third, capacity; fourth, understanding; fifth, knowledge; and last and least, experience. Without integrity, motivation is dangerous; without motivation, capacity is impotent; without capacity, understanding is limited; without understanding, knowledge is meaningless; without knowledge, experience is blind. Experience is easy to provide and quickly put to good use by people with all the other qualities.

Employing Yourself: Never hire or promote in your own image. It is foolish to replicate your strength. It is idiotic to replicate your weakness. It is essential to employ, trust, and reward those whose perspective, ability, and judgment are radically different from yours. It is also rare, for it requires uncommon humility, tolerance, and wisdom.

Compensation: Money motivates neither the best people, nor the best in people. It can move the body and influence the mind, but it cannot touch the heart or move the spirit; that is reserved for belief, principle, and morality. As Napoleon observed, "No amount of money will induce someone to lay down their life, but they will gladly do so for a bit of yellow ribbon."

Form and Substance: Substance is enduring, form is ephemeral. Failure to distinguish clearly between the two is ruinous. Success follows those adept at preserving the substance of the pat by clothing it in the forms of the future. Preserve substance; modify form; know the difference. The closest thing to a law of nature in business is that form has an affinity for expense, while substance has an affinity for income.

Creativity: The problem is never how to get new, innovative thoughts into your mind, but how to get old ones out. Every mind is a room packed with archaic furniture. You must get the old furniture of what you know, think, and believe out before anything new can get in. Make an empty space in any corner of your mind, and creativity will instantly fill it.

Leadership: Here is the very heart and soul of the matter. If you look to lead, invest at least 40% of your time managing yourself - your ethics, character, principles, purpose, motivation, and conduct. Invest at least 30% managing those with authority over you, and 15% managing your peers. Use the remaining time to inspire those you "work for" to understand and practice the theory. I use the terms "work for" advisedly, for if you don't understand that you should be working for your mislabeled "subordinates," you haven't understood anything. Lead yourself, lead your superiors, lead your peers, and free your people to do the same. All else is trivia.

things done to you that you abhorred. Don't do them to others, ever. Make another list of things done for you that you loved. Do them for others, always." You can read Hock's manual in summary form on the adjacent page.

Personal Leadership – to create the content

Jan Carlzon once said: "Those who have not been given the right information, cannot take responsibility. Those with the right information cannot help taking responsibility."

I define personal leadership as an extension of the mindset of those employees who, having been given the right information and support by a servant leadership, are responsible, active, independent and critical thinkers, say what they mean and contribute with the best they can offer. If they don't believe that the context created by a servant leadership can reach its goal effectively, then they speak out. This will mean that a facilitator can be brought in to mediate the relationship between leader and employees and adjust the context or content of production such that synergy is regained. However, the essence of the company's vision must not be changed so much that the company's overriding aim no longer exists, (unless that is, this vision is no longer relevant and it becomes necessary to draw up a new one.)

Personal leadership in no way opposes servant leadership because the employees know that their leaders want to serve their needs and help them to be the best they can. A company with both these functions will possess a high degree of trust, cooperation and fairness, or, in other words, a high degree of social capital. Both leaders and employees are in the same boat and are heading on the same course. Personal leadership shows a loyalty to the one leading, in the same way as the geese supported the goose flying upfront. Employees show cooperation and support for their leaders in an open and transparent environment.

A company model displaying these kind of qualities is in high demand from many leaders. This is a tendency confirmed in IBM's annual CEO analysis from 2012 which

"Know your limits - know yourself"

Who am I?	Identity	A person who has knowledge and respect for one's own, others', the company's and nature's interests and needs
Why is what I do important and which beliefs drive me?	Values	Authentic, non-exploitative, compassionate and non-judgemental
What is my potential / my competences?	Competences	The ability to express one's own interests and needs whilst also recognising and including others
How do I behave?	Behaviour	Show interest in others, and a wish to learn, connect and include
Which context do I create?	Environment	Create space for personal growth whilst respecting the whole

reports on 1700 CEO's from 64 countries and 18 business sectors across the globe. Directors are changing the way they work by adding qualities such as openness, transparency, and employee empowerment, to replace the traditional command and control systems that have otherwise defined their companies. According to IBM's research, the companies that lie ahead of their competition are 30% more likely to identify openness as an essential value base in their organisation. The most successful companies are implementing new models for the way they conduct their business, models which use the collective intelligence of the organisation and its network to discover new strategies for generating profit and growth. 53% of administrative directors have plans to use technology to facilitate a greater degree of partnering or cooperation with external organisations. 52% want to expand internal cooperation between different sectors of the organisation.

IBM concluded after this research that to build the next generation of workforce, an organisation must actively recruit and employ people who excel at working in open, team-based environments. At the same time, leaders must help their employees by assembling unconventional teams, adopting experienced-based learning, and by strengthening high-value employee networks.

Directors consider the following employee characteristics to be most vital for operating within a more complex and connected environment: interpersonal competences, such as cooperation (75%); communcation (67%); creativity (61%); and flexibility (61%). The tendency to demand greater cooperation stretches beyond the company itself to include external relationships. In a survey from 2008, over half of the directors contacted expressed an intention to develop more external partnerships, and in 2012 over two-thirds were making commitments along these lines.

These new tendencies - which reveal a belief, need, and will to cooperate - suggest an even greater demand for organisations to function as small dinghies at sea, bracing different tides and navigating in different directions. As such, we are moving away from the silos and towards new platforms. However, we still lack a new structure, or company model, which can support the movement. The two functions of servant leadership and personal leadership are both imperative for such a structure and model, and along with the facilitator, they make up the model's three core components.

The facilitator – creating connectivity and cohesion

To create a platform for sustainable growth requires a balance between what appears to oppose or be at loggerheads with each another: growth and sustainability; internal and external interests; and management and employees. We need to make sure that the friction between these dualities can be tolerated, just as a tight-rope walker uses a staff to aid her balance and keep herself on the rope. American anthropologist Gregory Bateson has said that "a person who walks is always out of balance." In the same way, a company in motion or transformation will always find itself in a state of imbalance, which its system must compensate for. This is why the third element is required in the new company model: namely, the facilitator. The facilitator ensures that the content stays within its context and that this context is conducive for its content. At the same time, facilitators are ambassadors for social capital - trust, cooperation, and fairness - ensuring that these elements are present and visible. They are also responsible for facilitating connections and cohesion within the organisation.

In contrast to the servant leader, who defines the direction and represents the flow, vision, and momentum, of the company, the facilitator has neither opinion nor stake in the context or the content. The facilitator function ensures that a good relationship is kept between the leadership and the employees by presenting observations to both parties without making hasty conclusions and without judging. The Indian philosopher, Jiddu Krishnamurti has said that the highest degree of intelligence is "to observe without judgment." The facilitator has the ability to do this and avoids trying to conclude on or decide a particular direction for the company. There, a water-tight lock balances the functions.

A metaphor for the facilitator is a *sailing master*. In the big sailing competitions, it is the captain of the boat who decides on its course whilst the crew do everything necessary to keep the boat moving forward as quickly and smoothly as possible. Between the captain and the crew stands a sailing master whose job it is to create a good cohesion between them. The sailing master does this by enabling an effective dialogue between captain and crew, making sure instructions are not issued too quickly and that the crew can keep up. The sailing master looks out to the horizon in the same direction as the captain whilst, at the same time, keeping his

"Be the role model you want around you"

Who am I?	Identity	A person who wants to create a balance between servant leadership and personal leadership
Why is what I do important and which beliefs drive me?	Values	Authentic, non-exploitative, compassionate and non-judgemental
What is my potential / my competences?	Competences	Knowledge about facilitation processes, active listening and systems. Empathy, impartial, balance
How do I behave?	Behaviour	Facilitates individuals and organisations to find common interests and needs
Which context do I create?	Environment	Inclusive and caring environment, open dialogue, respect for diversity

eyes on the crew. The sailing master or facilitator can be said to be Janus-faced, possessing the ability to see in two directions at once.

NOVO Nordic is one of few companies that have understood the importance of the facilitator function in ensuring cohesion and an integration of the whole. The company has fifteen full-time and twelve part-time facilitators employed under the sector of Business Assurance. Their job is to make sure that the context (in terms of the core values and leadership principles listed in the NOVO Nordic Way) come to life within the organisation (read more on page 173). The facilitators travel across the world between 75 countries to check whether the employees understand the context and intention behind their daily labour. If any team or unit from the 33.000 strong workforce is acting outside the context, it is then the facilitator's task to put them back on course and later check that the imbalance has gone for good. In doing this, the facilitator uses a process which, instead of telling employees what to do, supports them in discovering the right strategies for themselves, to allow the work they do to fit with Novo's context. The facilitators refer to what other areas in NOVO Nordic A/S have done to keep themselves on the platform.

Research conducted by Stanford professor in psychiatry, Irvin Yalom, concluded that people take responsibility for their own decisions and not others'. Socrates knew this intuitively. He was an advocate for thinking and acting in the same way. He believed that the most effective form of facilitation is that in which people discover their own solution and themselves take responsibility.

In his book *Existential Psychotherapy*, Yalom expresses it as follows: "In order to change oneself, one must first take responsibility; one must commit oneself with some form of action. Part of the word 'responsibility' means that one is obliged to make their 'response' to something or someone. The other part, 'ability' is a measure of how well one responds; how promptly and how effectively. Quite literally, responsibility is the ability to respond."

When I carry out a process of mediation in my work as a mediator, my starting point, like that of the facilitator, is to help people in taking personal responsibility for themselves rather than showing them what to do. Despite there being very few companies with a formal facilitator function, this doesn't necessarily mean that one doesn't exist in the company. Often the function is invisible and is only recognised when it is no longer around. Most of us can recall a colleague, whose job nobody is quite sure of and who isn't top of the list for selling most or contributing most over a certain period. But when this individual is no longer around, the atmosphere begins to get worse, trust starts to fracture, misunderstandings start to fester, and cooperation ceases.

"We realize that when we put our minds to it, we can develop technologies, organizations, political institutions and business models that allow us to prosper in ways that do not jeopardize Planet Earth. Collectively, we are approaching a state of global stewardship in which we manage our planet rationally, like any sensible landowner would his property."

Scenarie 1: "Man made World" from "In 100 Years – starting now", mindset-scenario for a sustainable society, ISSUES 2, House of Futures

"We realize that everything is nature, and so are we. We are one with Mother Earth, and we share a common biology and collective consciousness. On a deeper level, these are the sources of meaning that we all tap into, regardless of nationality, religion or culture."

Scenario 2: "Power of Nature" from "In 100 Years – starting now", mindset-scenario for a sustainable society, ISSUES 2, House of Futures

People can't put their finger on what has gone wrong. No one thinks that it is the person who left who had been facilitating the good cooperation, instilling trust and fairness in the group by asking questions, fulfilling people's needs, and telling others what they observe. Making the facilitator function visible, recognising it, and using it effectively in the system, creates a company in which all sectors can function together. This is necessary for achieving sustainable growth and for staying in balance whilst on the move.

A whole is made of three essences

The triple-function structure is based on natural design. It is well known to us in, for example, poetry, music, and system theory. One speaks of *The Rule of Three*, in which one unit appears as three constituent parts. We recognise the triple-function from expressions such as *being, having* and *doing*

- space, energy and *mass – man, woman and child - the father, the son and the holy spirit.* All these "families" are one substance but they consist of three essences or qualities. The origin of a line of thought is that a system functions best when it consists of three parts in relation to one another. If one of the parts is missing, the system cannot be optimised, and is therefore out of balance. This is supported by new research that shows that everything in life originates from one molecule, the RNA molecule, which contains genetic information and is self-replicating. The chemical structure of RNA is made up of three components; ribose sugars, bases and phosphates. RNA is a simplified version of DNA. People have been trying to put these elements together for the past forty years. It is only recently that Dr. John Sutherland from Manchester University has succeeded in doing so. All living things begin with the assembly of three components in whichever order makes the system function. This is why we have used a three-part structure to define the new company model for the platform. Montesquieu's tripartite division of power (i.e. executive, legislative, and judicial), which he devised under the French revolution over 250 years ago, must now be updated to a new tripartite system that better suits our present and our future. Montesquieu's tripartite system has been adopted by the entire Western world and is reflected also in the corporate world where we often see the legislative leader as, or at least part of, top leadership. Middle management, in turn, has the executive power, and judicial power is held by the audit and controller functions.

The new system, however, is an interest-based system that stems from the needs of the employees, the company and the surrounding community. Instead of having a legislative leader in the top post, we have a servant leadership. Instead of the executive power in middle management, we have personal leadership, and instead of the judicial power or controller, we have the facilitator. I call this system, The Butterfly Effect, because it is based on the law of nature, and as such, can be implemented as a natural transformation of what exists.

Servant Leadership
Context
Growth
Freedom
Healthy Competition
Systemic

Facilitator
Cohesion
Flexibility
Reciprocity
Collective spirit
Synchronisation

Personal Leadership
Content
Sustainability
Balance
Cooperation
Synergy

Audit controller
Without relations
Over burdened
Control
Fragmented
Separated in silos

**Command and
control management**
Growth and profit
Dominance
Rigidity
Exploitation
Abuse of power

Obedient subjects
Imbalance
Irresponsibility
Stagnation
Manipulation
Lack of power

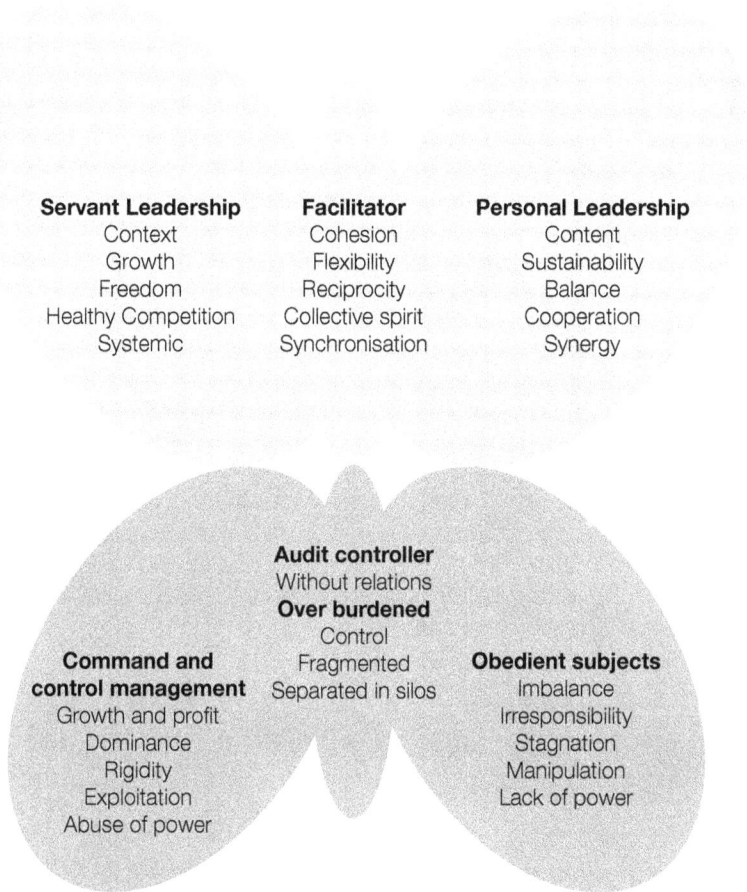

The Butterfly Effect – *Summary*

Figure 19 illustrates what I have covered in this book. The top butterfly is the new company model for creating sustainable growth; *The Butterfly Effect*. The bottom butterfly is the current model, or "shadow" side, which we must depart from for the good of both present and future generations.

INTRO

The interview on N.F.S. Grundtvig is about
the theologian and leader of one the greatest
movements in Scandinavia, the *folk school*
("højskole") movement. The author of the term,
servant leadership, Robert Greenleaf highlights
three examples of servant leaders. One of
these is Grundtvig. With Sune Auken's interview, you can get an insight into the qualities
present in his leadership. Sune Auken, PhD,
dr.phil is author, lecturer and one of Denmark's
leading authorities on Grundtvig. His doctoral
thesis is entitled *Saga's Mirror: Mythology,
History and Christianity According to N.F.S
Grundtvig* (2005).

Grundtvig as servant leader

It was only when Grundtvig was over 50 years old that he received any serious attention. Until this point, he had very few supporters. He had sufficient vision, but insufficient power to make anything materialize, and no one to stand behind him. However, towards the end of the 1830's, a series of events changed this situation and he rose from being the most meager man in the Danish kingdom to the most popular in a very short time. Without being granted any position of formal power, he nevertheless managed to become one of the most influential people of his time. When asked about Grundtvig's specific leadership qualities, Sune Auken refers to his ability "to lead from the head." Grundtvig always put himself on the line by leading at the very front of the people's movement he created. To lead from the head means that the army's general rides upfront in person, and as such, is the most vulnerable to attack. It isn't the wisest military tactic, but there does lie a clear leadership message in this courageous act. Such a leader moves the danger from his people to himself, thus taking any hits himself for the vision he bears. This requires a very different type of leader than then one who watches the battle through his telescope from a distant hill top and pulls back from the fight when their side begins to lose.

Leading from the head, as Grundtvig did, demands a particular strength of both physique and character, since one cannot hide behind others. Despite the lack of a formal position of authority, Grundtvig took leadership by inspiring others to follow him. He managed to communicate in a way that appealed to and captivated the many rather than only the few. Furthermore, he had a very particular, if not irregular, pedagogical talent. Even today, people know a suprisingly great deal about Grundtvig and what he stood for, and he can still fuse anger or enthusiasm under debate. This is quite an achievement from a distance of so many years.

Grundtvig was a man of the people, with wide appeal. He was neither withdrawn or cautious but carried an uncompromising manner and spoke his mind directly. He lacked any form of tact or affected tone. Whether they agreed with him or not, no one was ever in doubt of what Grundtvig stood for. On the other hand, Grundtvig was somewhat innocent, he thought the best of others until he was shown otherwise, and often made his exit in protest if he didn't get his way. He had qualities of being clear, authentic, inclusive and deeply honest.

As a leader, Grundtvig is remembered for his charisma and talent for public speaking, but he had great difficulty in starting a conversation with people he didn't know. Small talk was out of bounds for him. It was only when he was first underway with a speech that he could continue for hours. What most people don't know about Grundtvig is that he suceeded in finding a third way for bringing the people, the upper classes and the intellectual elite together. It is hard to associate him to one clear political persuasion. He always stood in opposition and it was a uphill challenge to bring him onboard any campaign that he hadn't initiated himself. His fundamental vision for society was to create a peaceful environment where the core element was people's ability to understand and work towards a shared goal which could benefit everyone. He was very preoccupied by the ability and dignity of people and the inevitability of having to acknowledge the stupidity and selfishness of others.

The movement that Grundtvig founded has had a profound impact on Denmark, but influence has also reached Sweden and, to an even greater degree, Norway. The Nordic countries differ from others in Europe and the rest of the world in that there are assembly centres, folk schools and churches which all host the people's discourse with a focus on the collective. This provides a conducive environment for dialogue and learning, where it is accepted that all dialogue must be in a language and tone which everyone can understand and react to, regardless of one's background in terms of class or education.

If one speaks in a way which is either over-intellectual or condescending in these venues, then one's speech is deemed to be a fiasco. As Sune Auken remarks: "One must communicate at eye-level and in a way which is clearly understood by all participants. Today's forms of leadership communication could learn a great deal from this in that they are often too elitist, prententious, patronising or loaded with jargon. Afterall, whatever cannot be understood and acknowledged, bears no meaning."

According to Sune Auken, it is Grundtvig's focus on equality in leadership that is his most important characteristic. This form of leadership is not only effective in producing positive visions, but resonates for all those listening. The value of leading without formal power is prevalent in Grundtvig's song, "*A balanced, joyful and active life on earth*". Via the words "(...) with equal worth in castle or hut", one sees the assets and interests of others as being equal to one's own despite perceived differences in social status. Grundtvig's ability to lead without power requires a humane approach, cohesiveness and a collective spirit - that which matters to you, also matters for me. It is with these values that the Nordic countries distinguish themselves from the rest of Europe and the world and it is with these values that Grundtvig based his form of leadership: a servant leadership. If we were more conscious of these values that define our culture, if we could take advantage of them and share our experience of how they can drive our companies, then we have a form of leadership which, from the front line, can motivate everyone to do their best for the collective and for the whole.

TO CARRY THE AIM IN ONESELF

Entelechy is a philosophical term created by Aristotle for describing the highest purpose or potential in processes of natural development. It is used to show that everything, in either form or nature, already bears a purpose despite this not having been realized or even detected. For example, an acorn bears all the characteristics for becoming an acorn tree.

According to Aristotle, everything strives to realize its entelechy in the same way as genes determine the growth of an organism. As such, entelechy is the expression of something's natural and inborn purpose.

CHAPTER 10

Tools for the three functions

I have assigned a particular tool to support each of the three functions of servant leadership, personal leadership and facilitation. For servant leadership, I introduce *dream sharing*, which is the ability to enable employees to dream the same dream and share the same vision as oneself. For personal leadership, I employ *protreptic coaching*, in which employees are coached with respect to their values and beliefs instead of their competences and behavior, which traditional coaching focuses on. For the facilitator function, I propose mediation as a process made up of five phases and which is inspired by natural decision-making processes.

#1: Dream sharing – a tool for servant leadership
In her book, "The Chalice and the Blade", Riane Eisler writes: *Despite us not usually giving it much thought, most social contexts; schools, hospitals, markets, political parties or churches are the result of ideas which once only existed in the minds of a few men or women. This is also the case when we consider the abolition of slavery, or the monarchy or other steps which have marked our social progression.*

The image of the future we want, drives the way we act. If leaders don't have a dream, then the only tools they have at their disposal are rewards or threats for "doing what is said." As indicated earlier in this book, such tools prove ineffective. But when a business leader describes a vision internally to the organisation, a change begins to occur amongst the employees. They are given a common focus of an overriding goal which all of them can work towards, each using their own competences. This creates committed employees who are passionate about their work and therefore act in the interests of the organisation.

I occasionally meet employees who are reprimanded for not showing enough passion, drive or motivation. I believe that it is the management, in the form of a servant leadership, who can best inspire passion in their employees by creating and sharing their own dreams. People are driven by neither carrot nor whip. The function of a servant leadership is to create a *pull* effect using an aim, a philosophy or a set of values that an employee can identify with and believe in, just as their leader does. The most important tool for a servant leader is to be able to share their dream with others and inspire them to follow this dream.

Dream sharing is not about preaching to others or assuming to know better than they do. As their leader, it is about getting your employees to see the same future as you do. When you see Columbus' ship out at sea, you need to describe it so clearly that your employees can eventually see it, too. Dream sharing is also about recognising that there are many ways of achieving the goal. It is therefore essential to trust one's employees and give them enough space to make their own decisions. Servant leadership creates the context but doesn't issue instructions or orders for how to reach the goal.

The context of servant leadership belongs to social constructivism. The way we perceive ourselves and others becomes our reality. In his book, *The Price of Inequality,* Nobel Prize winning economist Joseph Stiglitz describes an experiment in which Indian children from a low caste were put together with children from a high caste and asked to complete a task together without anyone knowing of the caste divide. In the experiment, the children contributed to the task in equal measures. Afterwards, the same task was repeated but this time, it was made clear who belonged to which caste. The result was that the children from the low caste performed a lot worse this second time around because in this reality they were defined as *the kids who weren't worth as much.*

"Fantasies are more than substitutes for unpleasant realities; they are also dress rehearsals, plans. All acts performed in the world begin with the imagination."

– Barbara Grizzuti Harrison

Images and perceptions of who we are, what we believe in, and what we are capable of, have a critical influence on whether or not we reach our goal. As Henry Ford said: "Regardless of whether you think you can, or you don't think you can, you are right."

Dream sharing is about creating a positive image that can inspire employees; one they can believe in and imagine, and one which appeals to their common sense and their emotions. In other words, it should appeal with *ethos, logos,* and *pathos.* Ethos describes the intitiator's credibility. Logos is the appeal to common sense, and pathos is the appeal to the recipient's emotions. It is important to have trust in the initiator because otherwise one cannot believe in what they say. In May 1961, U.S. President John F. Kennedy said: "First and foremost, I believe that this nation must commit to fulfilling the aim of a man landing on the moon and returning unharmed before the end of this decade." When Kennedy spoke of this dream and defined it as a common goal, then everyone worked together to make it happen. The rest is history: a space craft landed on the moon before the close of 1969 and Neil Armstrong spoke his famous words: "That's one small step for man, one giant leap for mankind."

A vision describes an ideal situation. It links what exists today to what can be created. Dream sharing is not to do with directing the process towards its goal, but keeping the goal visible to everyone. Kennedy didn't need to expand on how the rocket would be built, but simply state that the moon-landing was the vision. By using dream sharing, the leader invites their employees and partners to participate in the same dream.

To make it possible for employees to share one's dream, one needs to bring them into a new universe which they can see, hear, feel and understand. The communication of a servant leader's vision must be based on credibility, authenticity, openness and passion, in order to demonstrate that one believes in the vision oneself before sharing it. A good method is to use storytelling, but the stories need to be real for those listening. For example, a story can be told in the present tense, as if the employees were already there, living in the environment or situation that is desired. Effective ways to begin such a scenario are "imagine that…" or "think if it was the case that…" In general, it is also a good idea to write something down that can strengthen the intention.

One way to share one's dream with others is to create a common *vision-board* for the same dream. Visualising the dream in this way can be a strong reminder amid a busy daily routine, in which one can lose sight of the intended direction and how one had imagined contributing to it. *Figure 20* shows an alternative form of vision-board, a three-dimensional *Best in Class* mountain used in Michael Møllmann's mission for NOVO Nordic (read the interview on page 173).

#2: Protreptic coaching – a tool for personal leadership

The essence of personal leadership is an employee taking initiative to create the content to fit an agreed framework without being told what is right or wrong and without a detailed plan of how to do it. Therefore, we need a tool for engaging the employee towards responsibility and commitment and which can inspire them to discover *their own* strategies for fulfilling the aims. The tool is called *protreptic*.

Protreptic means directing the individual towards that which is most essential for themselves and their surrounding community. In this context, community is defined as the framework of values, visions and mission for driving the

company. Defining what is essential for the individual happens via a dialogue between a coach and the individual.

This way of practicing leadership goes back to the time of Aristotle. He made use of it in his leadership academy in Ancient Greece where one could follow a masters' course in protreptic coaching. Alexander The Great (356-323 B.C.) was inspired by both Cicero's and Aristotles' use of protreptic coaching and adopted it for himself and his closest leaders.

In doing so, he made sure that when his leaders set frameworks for others, they could instil them with the right values and beliefs and were able to communicate these effectively. His leaders were successful in acting quickly and in sync with each other, because they were conscious of their own values.

"He who has a why to live can bear almost any how."

– Friedrich Nietzsche

Alexander founded the city of Alexandria in Egypt, which, at the time, had the world's largest library and he managed to get people from the different nations under his rule to work with each other.

Professor of philosophy and leadership at Copenhagen Business School (CBS) Ole Fogh Kirkeby has revived the method for sharpening one's knowledge and values and describes it in his book, *Protreptic – philosophical coaching in leadership*. In a protreptic context, values are defined as the motives behind people's actions and the meaning behind these motives when they are conscious. It is our values and beliefs which drive us and which determine our everyday actions and behaviour. When we are conscious of our values we know exactly which decisions we need to take.

Protreptic makes it possible for a leader to become a servant leader. By focusing on values and by clarifying their meaning, employees can establish the necessary competences and behaviour for solving the task. Protreptic also makes it possible to define a common direction so that employees cooperate and work in the same flow. In protreptic coaching, the one being coached is asked to choose which servant leadership context or which values they want coaching in. The coaching occurs as an equal dialogue between the one coaching and the one being coached; for example, between a middle manager and an employee. Instead of offering advice, the coach will share experiences from their own life. The idea with the dialogue is that one can share thoughts and feelings with someone else and, in doing so, create a environment of trust and comfort.

"Keep it as simple as possible, but not simpler."

#3 Mediation – a tool for the facilitator

In their book, *The Power of Appreciative Inquiry*, Diana Whitney and Amanda Trosten-Bloom write the following: "Via conscious conversations and organisation design, one attempts to answer the question: What kind of organisation brings out the best in people, makes cooperation possible and contributes in demonstrating the highest values and ideals?"

Every time we make a decision, we go through a process which consists of five different phases (see figure 21 on page 217). None of these phases can be bypassed and one must follow them through in chronological order. Often we get stuck in a particular phase of the decision-making process which prevents us from moving forward. If we get stuck in this way, and cannot make contact with our needs, then we become disabled and unable to act.

The facilitator's tool is the process of natural decision-making. This creates connectivity and cohesion and supports the meeting between opposites. Researcher in psychology, Heather Cattell, PhD realised during an experiment in 1980 that people go through a certain thought sequence when they make decisions. This sequence or model can be used as a process of mediation. An introductory phase can be added in which all involved parties are asked to describe their experience of the situation. The facilitator doesn't come with a solution but works towards establishing a common ground between the parties, which puts them in the same phase, at the same time. What results from this is a parallel-process and a cooperation-process, which I describe in more detail in other books (see bibliography). The five phases in the mediation process are outlined as follows:

Phase 1: The parties involved should each tell their version of the story, how they have experienced the events, and what this has meant for them, without the mediator or anyone else judging whether what is said is right or not. Each person carries their own version of the truth, a version which is important for the others to hear and important for the individual to put into words. The purpose of this phase is to open up to one other and understand one another's intentions.

Phase 2: One must establish the needs, concerns and interests of those involved, and co-write a common description of the problem that can be used to find a solution. There may arise the need for someone to be listened to and involved in the decision-making process. There may be concerns that things are moving too quickly or too slowly. The purpose of this phase is to assist all parties in clarifying and articulating their needs and interests.

Phase 3: A common brainstorm is initiated in order to highlight a possible solution to the problem described. This should be able to meet the needs, concerns and interests of those involved. This phase is about establishing as many ideas as possible, regardless of whether or not they are realistic. Unrealistic ideas can often carry a solution. The purpose of this phase is to enable the different parties to understand that there are several solutions for satisfying one need.

Phase 4: Those involved determine which of the solutions from the brainstorm can be used. They then construct the basis of a common agreement outlining how they want things to be. The purpose of this phase is to offer support in choosing from the alternative possibilities.

FIGURE 21: THE MEDIATION PROCESS IN FIVE PHASES

	The five phases of the Mediation's Process	The natural decision-making process	Intention with the five phases	The prob-lems in the five phases
Phase 1	The parties articulate the problems openly and freely.		Open up to one another; understand the other's intention	Defence position; dis-comfort from confrontation
Phase 2	Establish un-fulfilled needs, concerns and interests – a common framing	Recognise an inner need. Take respon-sibility and mobilise the will	Go beyond set require-ments and help the parties in establishing the need	Not everyone knows how they feel, so they don't know what they want
Phase 3	Possible solutions are established via 'lateral thinking'; brainstorming	Fulfill the need. Establish the wants and possibilities	Equip the parties in un-derstanding that there are real solutions to fulfill the needs	Rigid and inflexible in one's under-standing / have difficulty in seeing pos-sibilities / low frustration threshold
Phase 4	The solution is chosen and an agreement is drawn up	Select the best possibilities – make a choice	Support the parties in choosing from the alternative possible solutions	Indecisive-ness / unreal-istic expecta-tions / lack of acceptance for not hav-ing all wants fulfilled
Phase 5	The agreement is signed off and an action plan drawn up	Implement the chosen solu-tion	Support the parties in drawing up a plan that can work for them	Poor self-discipline / difficulty in putting plans into action

Phase 5: The parties commit to the agreement and ensure that it is clear what needs to happen to solve the problem in a constructive way if the agreement no longer suits its purpose or if it needs adjusting in order to do so. The purpose of this phase is to develop a plan which can work for the parties involved.

You have now seen a company model built on flow, flex and form. You now also know the three functions which support these three essential components: servant leadership, facilitation and personal leadership. Finally, you have been given an insight of the three tools which support these three functions; dream sharing, mediation, and protreptic coaching. The one thing remaining, is a call to action in order to get you going. This is the objective of the book's final chapter.

TO DREAM

"I say to you today, my friends, so even though we face the difficulties of today and tomorrow, I still have a dream. It is a dream deeply rooted in the American dream. I have a dream that one day this nation will rise up and live out the true meaning of its creed: 'We hold these truths to be self-evident: that all men are created equal.' I have a dream that one day on the red hills of Georgia, the sons of former slaves and the sons of former slave owners will be able to sit down together at the table of brotherhood. I have a dream that one day even the state of Mississippi, a state sweltering with the heat of injustice, sweltering with the heat of oppression, will be transformed into the oasis of freedom and justice. I have a dream that my four little children will one day live in a nation where they will not be judged by the color of their skin but by the content of their character. I have a dream today."

– Martin Luther King in his speech of August 28th 1963

"Am I a person dreaming I'm a butterfly, or am I a butterfly dreaming I'm a person?"

– Lao Tse (ca. 300 BC.)

CHAPTER 11

Your vision for your company

This chapter covers how you can achieve a holistic overview of your company by combining the three elements of flow, flex, and form, or growth, connectivity, and sustainability, in a business model which can serve the company, the employees and society at large. In nature, transformation happens when cells respond relative to each other, and thereby create a new organism. Growth is organic and sustainable because it comes from the inside out and a new movement is initiated.

The first beating of wings

Greek-American evolutionary biologist, Dr. Elisabeth Sahtouris, has described a butterfly's metamorphosis from caterpillar to cocoon to butterfly as follows:

"When the larva (caterpillar) undergoes its transformation to a butterfly, small parts are created in the body of the larva which biological researchers call imaginary disks or imaginary cells. Since the larva's immune system cannot recognise these cells, it destroys them as soon as they are created. It is only when they begin to form links to each other that they become strong enough to resist the immune system. Eventually, the immune system is brought down under the process of transformation and the imaginary cells form the new body of a butterfly."

According to Sahtouris and the micro-biologist Mae-Wan Ho, life's existence is built from a self-organising and cooperative system in which every organism constantly upholds a balance between the interests of the group and the interests of the individual. The ability to support life in this way requires a *structure* which can take care of both the group's and the individual's interests. In an interest-based system, it is the cooperation between the one and the many which is key. As such, we move from an *either-or* mindset to a *both-and* mindset.

When companies develop from being a single-cell organisation to being self-organising organisms, then this creates a world of serendipity, with "happy coincidences and pleasant surprises." This puts focus on what we don't know and as such, cannot consciously seek, in the same way as the larva isn't conscious that it will become a butterfly.

More and more people believe that it is nature that can provide us with solutions to the many challenges that face us. It is only by learning from nature's design and by learning to cooperate with both nature and each other that we can survive long-term. The movement has already begun. Many examples of organisations and companies that have taken this route are described in this book and more are catching on everyday.

In nature, changes can occur so quickly that we often don't notice them happening. When studying weather and atmosphere, one uses the term, *The Butterfly Effect*, to describe how the beating of a butterfly's wings can cause small changes in the atmosphere which can finally result in a tornado occurring on the other side of the planet. The meteorologist Edward Lorenz, who was Professor at MIT, invented the Lorenz-attractor to predict the weather. This is a three-dimensional, non-linear structure that demonstrates long-term behaviour with respect to a chaotic flow. The Lorenz figure resembles a butterfly. The result is a dynamic system which develops over time as a complex, non-repetitive pattern, but we are not aware of the kind of serendipity that can be created. Nor do we know the precise moment in which a company starts to function and interact as a platform either internally or externally, with respect to its surrounding community.

The new imaginary cells are being transformed in today's society. I believe that those companies who are able to create a good, decentralised framework, with the freedom to think differently and facilitate clearly opposing beliefs between leadership and employees, will be the companies we want to dedicate our hearts and minds to. These are the companies who will have realised they must employ a model of sustainable growth in order to survive. This book is written in terms of flow, flex, and form, and is designed in our imaginary cells; that is, in our individual and social nature. In this design, development, cooperation, and existence are more important than an economic bottom line or any material value. It is not about getting faster, but better.

The end of the book is yours
Where is your company and organisation today? What do you want to pull down? What do you need to build up and then set free? What are you ready to transform in yourself? Which seeds will you and your company cultivate for the benefit of everyone and everything on earth? Which stories will be told in 100 years about the transformations which occur today?

I have collected different inspiration on the following pages, if and when you are ready to transform yourself and your organisation. Figure 22 on page 225 illustrates the platform as an organisation. It gives you an overview of what the platform consists of and it poses a series of questions that can help you to establish all the important factors. Furthermore, you can find links to videos which I find to be inspiring and thought provoking.

Before I send you out on your own journey, I would like to share a last quotation with you. The woman behind these words is Marilyn Schlitz, PhD, Senior Researcher at the Complementary Medicine Research Institute in California and Director of The Institute of Noetic Sciences, USA. She conducts research in the meaning of having common dreams. Her research has shown that when we dream and imagine together a reality which at first appears to be unattainable, then we can achieve the impossible. This research is based on The Ganzfeldt theory of common consciousness. According to Marilyn Schiltz:

"The implications are that we are all connected, and we criss-cross inside of each other. The data suggests that we are not these isolated beings, but in fact are all in a relationship at some core level. We dream together. We co-create together. We could move our consciousness from being a conversation about 'me' to being one that's about 'we', about our experience together. I think that this sends a really important message to people in America, and probably throughout the West, about our cult of narcissism and self-focus. Particularly now, when we're trying to come up with creative solutions to a better future for everyone, it's important to begin to think in these ways, about how we can co-dream and co-interpret in a way that's affirming."

It is my dream and intention to co-create the new infrastructure and movement for people who wish to lead with a holistic perspective and for the benefit of themselves, their company and their surroundings. The problems we face are the results of a fragmented way of thinking that can only be changed by an intelligent, collective spirit; one which can find, connect and support holistic solutions. I know that this dream will come true since more and more business leaders are in the process of major development, preparing themselves to orchestrate new platforms that can be set free.

Your dream

"It is my intention that_____

because_____

and because_____

I know that the dream will come true:

because_____

and because_____

Process based / systemic flow

Organism	*Identity*	Who are we as an organisation?
Life is like a kaleidoscope where all life can fulfil its full potential	*Values and beliefs*	Why is what we do important and what motivates us?
Learning, protreptic coaching, mediation and dream sharing	*Competences*	Which capacities are available to us as we work?
Supports the common good and higher purpose	*Behaviour*	How do we behave?
Chaos and change as in nature	*Environment and contextual conditions*	Which kind of environment are we creating?

Your notes:

_____

_____

_____

_____

_____

_____

Video links to inspire your process
See also the links on the website; *butterflyeffect.dk*

Planetary Collective: The Overview Effect
In 1987, the author, Frank White, described the experiences which transformed an astronaut's perspective of planet earth and its peoples' position in and on it. The common experience amongst astronauts is a feeling of respect and fear for our planet; a deep understanding of the link between life and a renewed feeling of environmental responsibility. You can learn more via these links:

- http://www.upworthy.com/some-strange-things-are-happening-to-astronauts-returning-to-earth?g=7/
- http://www.overviewthemovie.com/#!/watch/
- http://vimeo.com/55073825

Jeremy Rifkin: The Empathic Civilization
http://www.youtube.com/watch?v=l7AWnfFRc7g

Daniel Pink: The surprising truth about what motivates us
http://www.youtube.com/watch?v=u6XAPnuFjJc

Derek Sivers: How to start a movement
http://www.ted.com/talks/derek_sivers_how_to_start_a_movement.html

Flow in birds
http://www.youtube.com/watch?v=UdEjL9bVcCM

Simon Sinek: The Golden Circle
http://www.youtube.com/watch?v=l5Tw0PGcyN0

Jonas Gahr Støre: In Defense of Dialogue
http://www.ted.com/talks/jonas_gahr_store_in_defense_of_dialogue.html

Bibliography & Inspiration

Abbott, Edwin A.: *Flatland – A Journey of Many Dimensions*. Princeton University Press. 2008.

Amarasinha, Sascha; Larsen, Gitte; Monberg, Tina og Steenberg, Dorthe: *Common Ground*. Schønberg. 2009.

Amarasinha, Sascha og Kraul, Marie: *Klima kommunikation*. Gyldendal. 2009.

Bateson, Gregory: *Steps to an Ecology of Mind*. The University of Chicago Press. 1972.

Beck, Don og Cowan, Christopher: *Spiral Dynamics – Mastering values, leadership, and change*. Blackwell Publishing. 1996.

Belbin, Meredith: *Managing without Power*. Butterworth Heinemann. 2002.

Blanchard, Ken; Carlos, John og Randolph, Alan: *The 3 Keys to Empowerment*. Berret-Koehler Publishers 1999.

Block, Peter: *Stewardship – Choosing Service Over Self-Interest*. Berret-Koehler Publishers. 1996.

Bohm, David: *Thought as a System*. Routledge. 1994.

Borish, Steven M.: *The Land of the Living – The Danish folk high schools and Denmark's non-violent path to modernization*. Blue Dolphin Publishing. 1991.

Bragdon, Joseph (Jay) H. og Veatch-Bragdon, Jeanne: *Companies That Mimic Life: The New Profit Leaders,* Reflections, The SoL Journal, volume 8, number 2. 2007.

Branson, Richard: *Drop Business as Usual*. Gyldendal Business. 2013.

Campbell, David: *The Socially Constructed Organization*. Karnac. 2000.

Campbell, David, Coldicott, Tim og Kinsella, Keith: *Systemic Work with Organizations*. Karnac Books. 1994.

Carlzon, Jan: *Moments of Truth*. Harper. 1987.

Carse, James P.: *Finite and Infinite Games*. The Ballantine Publishing Group. 1986.

Csikszentmihalyi, Mihaly: *Finding Flow – The Psychology of Engagement with Everyday Life*. Perseus Book Group. 1997.

Csikszentmihalyi, Mihaly: *Flow – The Psychology of Happiness: The Classic Work on How to Achieve Happiness*. Harper Perennial Modern. 2002.

Diamond, Jared: *Collapse – How societies choose to fail or survive*. Penguin Books. 2005

Easwaran, Eknath: *Gandhi the Man – The story of His Transformation*. Nilgiri Press.1998.

Ellis, Tania: *The New Pioneers – Sustainable business success through social innovation and social entrepreneurship*. Wiley. 2010.

Ellsworth, Richard R.: *Leading with Purpose – The New Corporate Realities*. Stanford University Press. 2002.

Fukuyama, Francis: *Trust – The Social Virtues and the Creation of Prosperity*. Free Press Paperbacks.1995.

George, Bill: *Authentic Leadership – Rediscovering the Secrets to Creating Lasting Value*. Joessey-Bass. 2003.

Gleick, James: *Chaos – The Amazing Science of the Unpredictable*. Vintage. 1998.

Goleman, Daniel: *Emotional Intelligence*. Penguin Books. 2009.

Goleman, Daniel: *Følelsernes intelligens*. Borgen. 1997.

Gratton, Lynda: *Hot Spots*. Prentice Hall. 2007.

Greenleaf, Robert K.: *Servant leadership – A Journey into the Nature of Legitimate Power and Greatness*. Paulist Press. 1977.

Greenleaf, Robert K.: *The Power of Servant leadership*. Berrett-Koehler Publishers Inc. 1998.

Hamel, Gary: *The Future of Management*. Harvard Business Review Press. 2007.

Haque, Umair: *The New Capitalist Manifesto*. Harvard Business Review Press. 2011.

Hein, Helle Hedegaard: *Motivation*. Hans Reitzels Forlag. 2009.

Hildebrandt, Steen og Brandi, Søren: *Mangfoldighedsledelse*. Børsens Forlag. 2003.

Hildebrandt, Steen og Stubberup, Michael: *Bæredygtig ledelse – Ledelse med hjertet*, Gyldendal, 2010, og *Sustainable leadership*, foredrag den 8. juni, 2011, in100y.dk.

Hock, Dee: *One from Many*. Berrett-Koehler Publishers Inc. 2005.

Hsieh, Tony: *Delivering Happiness – A Path to Profits, Passion and Purpose*. Business Plus. 2010.

Hubbard, Barbara Marx: *Conscious Evolution – Awakening the Power of Our Social Potential*. New World Library. 1999.

ISSUES 2: *This way, please! Preferred Futures 2112*, House of Futures, april 2012.

Jensen, Claus: *Challenger – et teknisk uheld*. Samleren. 1993.

Kim, W. Chan og Mauborgne, Renée: *Blue Ocean Strategy*. Børsens Forlag. 2005.

Kinsley, Michael: *Creative Capitalism*. Simon and Schuster. 2008.

Kuhn, Harold W. og Nasar, Sylvia: *The Essential John Nash*. Princeton University Press. 2002.

Laszlo, Ervin: *Science and the Akashic Field*. Inner Traditions. 2007.

Laszlo, Ervin: *The Chaos Point – The World at the Crossroads*. Piatkus. 2009.

Laszlo, Ervin: *WorldShift 2012 – Making Green Busines, New Politics & Higher Consciousness Work Together*. Inner Traditions. 2010.

Lax, David A. og Sebenius, James K.: *The Manager as Negotiator – Bargaining for Cooperation and Competitive Gain*. The Free Press. 1986.

Loehr, Jim: *The Power of Story*. Free Press. 2007.

Mackey, John: *Passion and Purpose – The Power of Conscious Capitalism*. Sounds True. CD. 2009.

Maslow, Abraham Harold: *Toward a Psychology of Being*. John Wiley & Sons Inc. Third edition, 1999.

Maslow, Abraham Harold: *Maslow on Management*. John Wiley & Sons Inc. 1998.

McTaggart, Lynne: *The Bond – Connecting through the Space Between Us*. Hayhouse. 2011.

Miller, Peter: *Smart Swarm – Using Animal Behaviour to Change our World*. Collins. 2010.

Monberg, Tina: *To vindere*. Børsens Forlag. 2002.

Monberg, Tina: *Handbook of Human Conflict Technology*, Paragon Publishing, 2009

Monberg, Tina: *Konfliktens redskaber*. Børsens Forlag. 2005.

Monberg, Tina: *Konflikthåndtering*. Børsens Forlag. 2006.

Nash, John F., jr.: *Essays on Game Theory*. Edward Elgar. 1996.

Nair, Keshavan: *Beyond Winner – The handbook for the leadership revolution*. Paradox Press. 1990.

Oshry, Berry: *Seeing Systems, Unlocking the Mysteries of Organizational Life*. Berret-Koehler Publishers 2007.

Pink, Daniel: *A whole New Mind – How to thrive in the new conceptual age*. Cyan. 2005.

Pink, Daniel: *Drive – The surprising truth about what motivates us*. Canongate. 2011.

Petersen, Verner C.: *Hinsides regler*. Børsens Forlag. 2004.

Prigogine, Ilya: *The End of Certainty – Time, Chaos and the New Laws of Nature*. The Free Press. 1997.

Putnam, Robert D.: *Bowling Alone – The Collapse and Revival of American Community*. Simon & Schuster Paperbacks. 2000.

Rifkin, Jeremy: *The Empathic Civilization – The Race to Global Consciousness in a World in Crisis*. Polity Press. 2009.

Scharmer, Otto C.: *Theory U – Leading from the Future as It Emerges*. Berret-Koehler Publishers. 2009.

Schumacher, E.F.: *Small is Beautiful – A study of economics as if people mattered*. 1993. Vintage Books.

Scott-Morgan, Peter: *The Reality of Global Crisis*. 2012.

Scott-Morgan, Peter: *The Reality of our Global Future*. 2012.

Schutz, Will: *The Truth Option*. Ten Speed Press. 1984.

Semler, Ricardo: *Maverick!*. Random House. 1993.

Senge, Peter: *The Fifth Discipline*. Random House. 1999.

Sheldrake, Rupert: *The Hypothesis of a New Science of Life*. Park Street Press. 1987.

Sheldrake, Rupert: *Seven Experiments That Could Change the World*. Fourth Estate. 1995.

Sharma, Robin: *The Leader Who Had No Title*. Simon & Schuster. 2010.

Smith, Adam: *Wealth of Nations*. J.M. Dent & Sons Ltd. 1954.

Strong, Michael: *Be the Solution – How Entrepreneurs and Conscious Capitalists Can Solve All the World's Problem*. Wiley. 2009.

Taleb, Nassim Nicholas: *The Black Swan – The Impact of the Highly Improbable*. Random House. 2007.

Tillich, Paul: Love, *Power and Justice*. Oxford University Press. 1954.

Torekull, Bertil og Ingvar Kamprad: *Historien om IKEA*, ABC Forlag, 2007.

Torekull, Bertil: *Kamprads lilla gulblå*, Ekerlids Forlag, 2011.

Varela, Francisco J. og Matura, Humberto R.: *The Tree of Knowledge*. Shambhala. 1998.

Wallander, Jan: *Budgeten – ett onödigt ont*. SNS Förlag. 1995.

Wallander, Jan: *Med den mänskliga naturen – inte mot!*. SNS Förlag. 2002.

Westley, Frances, Zimmerman, Brenda og Quinn Patton, Michael: *Getting to Maybe*. Vintage Canada. 2007.

Wheatley, Margaret J.: *Leadership and the New Science*. Berret-Koehler Publishers. 1999.

Wheatley, Margaret J.: *Finding Our Way*. Berret-Koehler Publishers. 2005.

Wheatley, Margaret J.: *So far from Home*. Berret-Koehler Publishers. 2012.

Waal, Frans de: *The Age of Empathy – Nature's lessons for a kinder society*. Souvenir Press. 2009.

Yalom, Irvin D.: *Eksistentiel psykoterapi*. Hans Reitzels Forlag. 2000.

Glossary

Alignment

A parallel process created between different parties in order to establish a working collaboration.

Butterfly Effect

The Lorenz attractor is a three dimensional geometric structure used in chaos theory to show the behaviour in a chaotic flow. The structure has the form of a butterfly and is therefore named The Butterfly Effect. The Butterfly Effect is also a company model which consists of three functions in the form of servant leadership, personal leadership and facilitation.

Movement

A dynamic organisation's structure which can use its resources to find, connect and support those who share the same purpose in order to reach a better overall result.

Black Swan

Described by Nassim Nicholas Taleb as the case of analysing something in detail only to discover afterwards that we have missed the most essential point or part. We see white swans but not the black ones. If we don't believe in something then we can't see it, and therefore we can't measure it.

Command and control

Systems and management methods in which management is formed by issuing orders and rules for what employees should do, and afterwards checking the extent to which orders have been carried out.

Dream Sharing
The ability to enable employees to dream the same dream or share the same vision for the purpose of achieving a specific goal. Dream sharing is the tool of a servant leader, used to create a positive image which employees can believe in as a result of it appealing to their feelings, senses and concerns.

Emergence
A condition in which the finished result becomes greater than the individual parts. Often the consequence of an effective working collaboration between people and companies.

Engagement
An "engaged employee" is one who is fully involved and enthusiastic with regard to their work and their organisation's vision. As a result of this engagement, they behave in a way which directly benefits the interests of the organisation.

Facilitator
The function or mechanism which creates cohesion between an organisation's context and the content made by the employees. The facilitator function is responsible for cohesion and flex. Those employees who facilitate others are named as facilitators. The facilitator is one of the three key functions in The Butterfly Effect model.

Fellowship
A form of commitment in which employees are drawn to follow a particular leader once it is evident that the leader actively serves both their own and the groups' common interests.

Forecast
To predict the most likely future based on projections and prognoses.

Geronimo Coefficient
Shows how decentralized a structure is and, as such, the ex-

tent to which power and responsibility are evenly distributed throughout an organisation. At the same time, this should ensure that the difference between the highest and lowest paid salaries never gets too large.

Critical mass
The number of individuals it takes to make change possible. Once ten per cent of a population hold the same stable belief or conviction, then this will always be accepted by the majority of the population.

Mediation
A five-phase facilitation process based on natural decision-making processes. Download a free app of the mediation process here;

Partnership
Developed to strengthen the collaboration between two or more parties early on in a development process and using common goals, a common organisation and setting common economic interests. The form of cooperation is based on a trust in, and focus on a superordinate goal for creating a higher value within the project. A strategic partnership agreement, or similar commitment, is drawn up dependent on the needs and wants of both parties. The best partnerships are those which result in equal quality, satisfaction and success being felt by both or all parties. This is referred to as a *"win-win"* result.

Personal leadership
Having responsibility for the content, knowledge and/or competence necessary in a particular work task in order to fulfil the set goal. Personal leadership ensures balance, content to the context, and as such, the form the project or

process should take. Personal leadership is one of the three functions in *The Butterfly Effect* model.

Platform
A horizontal organisation structure which is cohesive in that there is good synergy between two or more employees, products and / or ideas. In the book, the platform is described as the opposite to the silo which has a vertical and hierarchical structure.

Protreptic coaching
A tool for personal leadership developed by Professor Ole Fogh Kirkeby of Copenhagen Business School. In protreptic coaching, employees are coached on their values and beliefs, rather than their competences and behaviour as is the case in traditional coaching.

Serendipity
A happy coincidence or a pleasant surprise.

Servant leadership
Employees who create the platform's context as a resource and create the possibility for contributing to growth. The term was created by Robert Greenleaf in 1970 when referring to a leader whose first interest lies in serving collective needs and second, in being leader. Such a leader first *becomes* a leader once they have articulated a clear vision for serving the common good. Servant leadership creates flow. Servant leadership is one of the three functions in The Butterfly Effect model.

Silo
The silo creates comfort and foresight since it divides and simplifies conditions which can otherwise appear to be unfathomable. Such divisioning, gives a leader an organised and apparently simpler position from which to manage and control the tasks being carried out in the separate departments. According to the chief argument of this book, silos

carry key negative characteristics of not being able to support flow, sustainability or cohesion.

Superordinate goal

A goal that is big enough and convincing enough to allow individuals and groups to overcome personal differences for the sake of achieving something more essential which lies beyond their own reach. A superordinate goal has two prerequisites which both need to be in place in order to mobilise the employees and the leadership. Firstly, everyone must agree on the goal, meaning that it must be both appealing and make sense to everyone. Secondly, the goal can only be reached by everyone contributing and cooperating.

Swarm

A swarm's behaviour is reminiscent of a self-organising system. The control structure is decentralized, the challenge is distributed across everyone present, and multiple interactions occur between all individuals. When these three mechanisms occur at the same time, then a group of employees in a company can tackle and complete a task via a decisive pattern of collective actions, without being preprogrammed or told what to do.

About the author

Tina Monberg (1961)

Tina Monberg is partner at *Mediationcenter A/S* and expert in handling conflicts and collaborations in business via mediation and with a focus on human relations.

Tina has a multi-disciplinary background as mediator, lawyer and psychotherapist. She has twenty years experience in teaching and advising businesses, organisations and leaders in new types of business relations. These include; sustainable partnerships, holistic organisation structures and interest-based conflict solutions. Tina is an international keynote speaker in high demand and author of five books on mediation and cooperation. She has recently developed, *The Butterfly Effect*; a new concept for organisation and leadership.

Read more about The Butterfly Effect at butterflyeffect.dk, tinamonberg.dk and mediationcenter.dk or contact Tina directly by email tm@mediationcenter.dk or phone +45 20 47 82 28.

About the editor

Gitte Larsen (1970)

Gitte Larsen is an author, editor and futurist. After thirteen years at the Copenhagen Institute for Future Studies (*Instituttet for Fremtidsforskning*), eight of which spent as editor-in-chief for prize-winning magazine FO (future orientation / fremtidsorientering), Gitte founded editorial consultancy, *Editions* and in collaboration with a series of other companies, *House of Futures*, for which she is currently managing director and founding partner.

Gitte designs and directs large development and communication projects including *In 100 Years – starting now* (2010-2012), which resulted in the conception and realisation of a new centre for sustainability and resilience for Denmark.

Gitte is the author of a number of books and articles and is a well-known keynote speaker on subjects including; future economics, future business, sustainable society development and women in leadership.

Read more at editions.dk, houseoffutures.dk and in100y.dk. Contact Gitte directly by email gitte@houseoffutures.dk or phone +45 20 21 11 47.

Thanks to

I would like to express my heartfelt gratitude to all who have contributed to this book and who have inspired me over the past ten years during dialogue, teaching and collaborations.

In particular, I would like to thank:

Jan Carlzon, Michael Møllmann, Sune Auken and *Jan Wallander* for sharing their insights, wisdom and knowledge.

Gitte Larsen, futurist, editor and partner at Editions and House of Futures for your support and structure. Without your ongoing affection, this book would never had materialised.

Erik, my husband, and my children *Philip* and *Cecilia* for putting up with me despite my absence from family-time.

A special and heartfelt thank you to to *Stine Skøtt Olesen* for creating illustrations and layout in flow, flex and form and to *Dominic Balmforth*, the midwife of this English translation. You worked magic in finding the perfect words to embody the spirit and the concepts I wanted to bring to the world - thank you.

www.ingramcontent.com/pod-product-compliance
Lightning Source LLC
Chambersburg PA
CBHW071542200326
41519CB00021BB/6585